Healing Plants of the Bible

HISTORY, LORE & MEDITATIONS

VINCENZINA KRYMOW

Illustrated by
A. JOSEPH BARRISH, S.M.

With meditations by
M. JEAN FRISK

NOVALIS

WILD GOOSE PUBLICATIONS
www.ionabooks.com

ST. ANTHONY MESSENGER PRESS
Cincinnati, Ohio

Scripture citations are taken from the *New Revised Standard Version of the Bible,* copyright ©1989, by the Division of Christian Education of the National Council of the Churches of Christ in the U.S.A. Used by permission. All rights reserved.

Cover and book design by Constance Wolfer

ISBN 0-86716-467-0

Library of Congress Cataloging-in-Publication Data

Krymow, Vincenzina.
  Healing plants of the Bible: history, lore, and meditations / by
Vincenzina Krymow; illustrated by A. Joseph Barrish; with meditations
by M. Jean Frisk.
      p. cm.
Includes bibliographical references.
  ISBN 0-86716-467-0 (hardcover)
  1. Plants in the Bible. 2. Medicinal plants—Palestine. 3. Plants in
the Bible—Meditations. 4. Medicinal plants—Religious
aspects—Christianity—Meditations. 5. Historic gardens—Guidebooks.
I. Title.
  BS665 .K79 2002
  220.8'581634—dc21

                                  2002000291

Published by St. Anthony Messenger Press
www.AmericanCatholic.org

———————————————

Published in Canada by
Novalis
49 Front Street East, 2nd Floor
Toronto, Ontario, Canada
M5E 1B3
Phone: 1-800-387-7164 or (416) 363-3303
Fax: 1-800-204-4140 or (416) 363-9409
E-mail: cservice@novalis.ca

A catalogue record of this book is available from the National Library
of Canada.

ISBN: 2-89507-242-6

———————————————

UK edition first published 2002 by
Wild Goose Publications
Fourth Floor, Savoy House, 140 Sauchiehall Street, Glasgow G2 3DH, UK
www.ionabooks.com

Wild Goose Publications is the publishing division of the Iona Community.
Scottish Charity No. SCO03794. Limited Company Reg. No. SCO96243.

ISBN 1 901557 67 7

A catalogue record for this book is available from the British Library.

Distributed in New Zealand by
Pleroma, Higginson Street, Otane 4170, Central Hawkes Bay, New Zealand.

Table of Contents

Dedicated to

my husband, Joachim,

and

my grandson, Jacob.

Acknowledgments

The author would like to thank the many biblical botanists, scholars and gardeners whose work informed her knowledge and understanding of healing plants of the Bible; herbalists Martha Martin and Trish Zeh for their ideas and suggestions and for the loan of numerous reference materials; Jennifer Shrubsole and the other reference librarians at the Washington-Centerville Public Library for their help in researching obscure references and obtaining rare books from other libraries; Father Johann Roten, S.M., Father Thomas Thompson, S.M., and the staff at the Marian Library, University of Dayton, for their encouragement and assistance; the Mariological Society of America for the generous award from the Clinton Fund for travel to biblical sites and biblical gardens; and her husband for proofreading and for his patience and understanding.

Introduction

Solomon "would speak of trees,
from the cedar that is in the Lebanon
to the hyssop that grows in the wall..."
—1 Kings 4:33

The wise king Solomon, perhaps the first botanist of the Bible, knew his vegetation well. The Song of Solomon contains references to twenty-three plants and their products. Most of the flora mentioned—grapes, palms, figs, myrrh, aloes, saffron and lilies—are used for healing. Jotham, the other botanist mentioned in the Bible, describes the fruits of the olive and fig trees and the grapevine (Judges 9:7–15).

In Deuteronomy we read that Israel was blessed with seven life-sustaining plants. It was a "land of wheat and barley, of vines and fig trees and pomegranates, a land of olive trees and honey..." (8:8). The honey referred to here is the nectar of the date palm tree.

Hundreds of verses in the Old and New Testaments mention more than a hundred different kinds of plant life. Allusions to trees, shrubs, herbs and flowers would have come easily to the people of the Bible. The early inhabitants of the Promised Land lived mostly in the valleys and plains, where plenty of water and rich soil fostered the development of agriculture. For the mostly pastoral and agrarian Hebrews, vineyards and olive groves were valuable assets. Their fields and forests yielded not only food but also products for making cloth, building structures and treating many common ailments.

Plant life was part of daily life. Tithes were set for the products of the land, daily offerings of crops were burned on the altar of the Temple, bitter herbs were required for the Passover feast and four different plants were part of the Sukkoth celebration.

In Scripture healing was associated with faithfulness and belief in the power of God. In the Old Testament God healed Abimelech and his wife and female slaves (Genesis 20:17) and the faithful Hezekiah (2 Kings 20:5). The Lord listened to the supplications of those in Egypt and healed them (Isaiah 19:22). During his ministry Jesus healed the body by healing the spirit. He cast out devils and unclean spirits and restored to wholeness those who believed in God.

Even though there are only a few references to the medicinal use of plants in the Bible, the Israelites, during their long servitude in Egypt, would have learned about this method of healing from the Egyptians. They would have taken this knowledge, together with the herbs and plants, with them when they left. The aloes, herbs and fruits mentioned in the Bible are still valued for their healing properties.

Biblical plants interested such ancient botanists as the Greek Theophrastus and Roman Pliny, but it was not until 1566 that the first book dealing entirely with plants mentioned in Scripture was published. The pioneering work of Flemish physician Levinus Lemnius was followed by several books in the seventeenth century, mostly based on the authors' knowledge of plants growing in Europe. In 1757 the "Immortal Swede" Carolus Linnaeus published the results of his student Hasselquist's two-year exploration of the flora of Egypt and Palestine. Biblical botanists since then have debated the correct identification of the plants mentioned in Scripture. Most now agree that lilies of the field are not lilies, anise is dill and the apple was probably an apricot.

More recently, botanists have begun to explore the medicinal value of plants mentioned in the Bible. Growing interest in holistic health and natural remedies has sparked a renewed interest in the ancient uses of plants for healing. Folk remedies cast aside with the advent of pharmaceuticals are once again being used. Aromatherapy uses the healing power of flower essences to correct imbalances of body, mind and spirit; homeopathy relies on the essence of plant substances to stimulate the healing inner resources of the body. Herbalists use time-honored formulas for treating modern-day ailments. Meditating on the symbolism of flowers and herbs renews the spirit and brings us closer to the universal spirit, God.

The purpose of this book is to offer information about the healing plants of the Bible and their scriptural contexts, their uses in biblical times, their present-day uses and their roles in healing body, mind and soul. *Healing Plants of the Bible* does not provide prescriptions for use of the plants for healing and urges readers to consult trained practitioners for professional guidance.

About This Book

The first part, Land of the Bible, tells about the plants of the Bible lands, then and now. It describes many of the difficulties encountered in identifying these plants—biblical references are sometimes vague and translation errors do occur. It also gives information about the climate of the Holy Land and the vegetation in the five geographic zones: the Mediterranean coastal plain, the hill country, the Jordan rift valley, the Transjordan plateau and the desert zone.

Medicine and healing in biblical times is the subject of the second section. It recounts the role of God and the temple priests in healing and tells how Jesus healed the sick. It presents evidence that the herbalists of Hebrew, Egyptian and Assyrian cultures were well versed in the use of native plants for healing. Further, it discusses the symbolism of some of the healing plants as used in biblical references.

Part three presents thirty-eight biblical plants. For each plant a biblical reference is given, together with information about its history, lore and use. The plants are arranged in twelve kindred groups: tithing herbs, bitter herbs, lilies of the field and valley and so on. An original illustration of each plant by Marianist brother and artist A. Joseph Barrish and a meditation by M. Jean Frisk, Schoenstatt Sister of Mary, accompany the text for each plant.

Part four starts with a brief review of gardens in the Bible, beginning with the Garden of Eden and ending with the garden in Revelation. A brief discussion of the importance of Scripture gardens is followed by descriptions of thirty-six Scripture gardens in the United States, Canada, Israel and Great Britain, with information for visiting them. A final section has suggestions for planting a Scripture garden.

The appendix discusses an additional forty plants not previously treated, with biblical references and facts about the plants' uses.

PART ONE

Land of the Bible

*"The Lord said to Moses,
'Send men to spy out the land of Canaan,
which I am giving to the Israelites.'"*
—*Numbers 13:1–2*

From Deuteronomy we get a glimpse of this land of the Bible: "For the Lord your God is bringing you into a good land, a land with flowing streams, with springs and underground waters welling up in valleys and hills, a land of wheat and barley, of vines and fig trees and pomegranates, a land of olive trees and honey" (8:7–8). Nearby were also deserts: "the great and terrible wilderness, an arid wasteland" (8:15).

The earliest settlers lived mostly in the valleys and plains, where water was plentiful and the soil was rich. Wild thickets and forests covered the surrounding hills and slopes. When the children of Israel entered the Promised Land, they began the difficult task of clearing the wild, uncultivated hills. Joshua 17:15 tells the tribe of Joseph to "go up to the forest, and clear ground" for themselves.

Changes in the Land

Over the centuries the landscape changed and the once-fertile land became barren. Forests were cleared to provide timber and fuel. Shepherds burned woodlands, replacing trees with herbaceous plants to improve pasturing for their goats and sheep. In other areas overgrazing stressed existing flora and allowed penetration by foreign species. Soil erosion devastated the land as ancient terrace-type cultivation was abandoned. At one time landowners cut down trees to avoid paying taxes for them to the Romans, and successive hordes of invaders further destroyed the land.

Since 1948 the government of Israel has implemented a program that includes protecting endangered species, reforesting the land and draining swamplands in the north to provide land for agriculture.

Climate and Vegetation

There are two seasons in the land of the Israelites: summer and winter. Summers are hot and dry, with east or desert winds predominating. Winters are cool and wet, with rainfall decreasing from north to south. Transitional months of September and October lead into the rainy season; in March and April the rains taper off.

Meteorologists speak of three climatic zones. The Mediterranean, or temperate, zone along the coastal plain has dry, fairly hot summers and winter rainfall of twenty to forty inches per year, beginning in late September or early October and ending in April. The rainy winter season is the peak growing time for crops, fruiting time for orchards and blossoming time for many of the flowers. Humidity is high and in the summer dew collects at night, providing moisture for the plants.

The Irano-Turanian Steppe zone, separating the Mediterranean zone from the desert zone, is semiarid with long periods of dryness and barely ten inches of rain between December and March. Bulbous plants that store nutrients in their corms or bulbs, trees and shrubs that shed their leaves during the dry months and quick-blooming annual flowers flourish here, covering the land with foliage and color in winter and spring.

The desert zone of the Samarian and Judean deserts and the Negev is hot and arid, with nominal rainfall of less than four inches. Few plants grow here, and only when rain comes over a period of time instead of in a sudden deluge. A subzone, called the Sudanese, consists of oases, islands of vegetation in the desert thought to be relics of ancient tropical jungles. The occasional date palm tree is found here.

Jericho desert

Geography and Plant Life

The lands mentioned in the Bible extend from Italy to Iran and from Greece to Egypt, but most of the biblical events occurred in the area called the land of Israel, or Palestine, on both sides of the River Jordan.

At the southern tip of the area known as the Fertile Crescent lies the land of Canaan, as it was called in biblical times. With the Mediterranean Sea to the west, mountains in the north and deserts to the east and south, this narrow strip of land, smaller than the state of New Hampshire, was blessed with fertile valleys, mild temperatures and adequate rainfall. Hills and mountains, valleys and plains, rivers, lakes, deserts and oases covered the region and the terrain changed dramatically from west to east and north to south.

Botanists speak of five distinct geographic regions of Palestine. The coastal plain, with its sand dunes, lush meadows and fertile soil, lies between the Mediterranean Sea and a hilly plateau to the east. The coastal plain runs 140 miles south from Lebanon, from Mount Carmel to Gaza. In the north tulip and storax bushes bloom in the spring and mandrakes in the winter. Low-growing herbs with small, fleshy or hairy leaves designed to hold water grow in the sandy areas. White sand lily is one of the first flowers to blossom along the Mediterranean coast at the end of a long, hot, dry summer. Carob trees and Kermes oak dominate forests of the coastal plains. Lily, hyacinth, anemone, iris and crocus grow inland.

Eastward is the central hill country, alternating hills and plateaus. It includes the valley of Jezreel, the Judean hills to the east and the hills of southern Galilee and Samaria and extends for 160 miles from Dan at the foot of Mount Herman to Beersheba, where the desert begins. In biblical times oaks, terebinths and Judas trees covered the woodland slopes to the west. Now several varieties of oak trees grow in the woodlands, areas where logging and other practices have disturbed growth. Cyclamen, rockrose, thorn apple, sage and wormwood grow in areas of less dense growth known as *garrigues* and *bathas*. Bay laurel grows in upper Galilee, and almond trees thrive near Mount Tabor. Carob trees grow wild in the mountains, and the slopes are terraced for olive trees and vineyards. In the south blessed thistle and crown daisies flourish.

Called the "Descender," the Jordan River rushes down from the Banias Spring at the foot of Mount Hermon into the Hulah Basin, flows on until it reaches the Kinneret, or Sea of Galilee, and meanders until it empties into the Dead Sea, the lowest spot on earth. The Jordan River Valley extends down the middle of Palestine for 165 miles, forming part of the rift valley, which stretches from Syria to Africa. Wilderness and the salty "badlands" along the Jordan have been transformed into fertile fields. Poppies and tulips bloom on Mount Hermon. Oleander grows along streams, and papyrus thrives in the Hula Nature Reserve. Red anemone, cyclamen and crown daisies are among the wildflowers growing near the Sea of Galilee, and forests of tamarisk trees grow along the river.

East of the Jordan a high tableland, the Transjordan plateau, rises sharply. In the north are the Golan Heights, formed by ancient volcanic eruptions.

Hill country

9

Southward, in the land of Gilead, woodlands have been cleared and fertile hills are covered with olive groves and vineyards. Three rivers slice through the area: The Yarmuk and the Jabbok flow into the Jordan, and the Arnon drains into the Dead Sea. Semishrubs of wormwood and woody ferns grow here, and in moist years tulip, iris, buttercup and anemone bloom in the steppes. Farther south are the red cliffs of Edom.

To the south are the sand dunes and rocky cliffs of the Negev Desert. Mountain lily, Negev iris and desert tulip are found in the northern Negev. In the east the Judean Desert is volcanic in nature, with lava flows forming small hills. Most of the vegetation is confined to oases and wadis. Acacia and mastic trees, white broom and thistle grow in some areas.

Plants in the Bible

Most of the plants named in the Bible are native to Egypt and Palestine. Some, mainly those producing incense and spices, were imported from Arabia, Ceylon and India via established trade routes. The Old and New Testaments mention more than 125 different plants, and hundreds more are found in the Hebrew Mishna, Talmud and Midrashim.

New plants have been introduced over the centuries, and biblical botanists estimate that today there are at least 126 families of plants, 850 genera or classes and from 2,300 to 3,500 species or specific types of plants in Israel. Since the general climatic conditions of the country have changed little since biblical days, many of the native plants still exist. Mediterranean flora is one of the most varied and abundant in the world.

Archaeologists have found that the plants and plant product remains in excavations do not differ much from the present-day variety. Remains of garlic, leeks and onions, pomegranates and dates have been found in the caves of Nahal Mishmar near the Dead Sea. Olive pits have been discovered in various excavation sites surrounding the Dead Sea. Garlands of celery leaves and white lotus petals were found in mummies from about 1000 B.C. in Egypt.

Identification of the plants mentioned in the Bible has posed problems for biblical botanists and scholars. Several factors contributed to the difficulty. The writers of the Bible were not botanists and often spoke in general terms, such as using "lilies of the valley" for hyacinth and iris, "lilies of the field" for anemone. Some plant names were used for more than one species, such as *erez* (cedar) for the true cedar, the pine, tamarisk and probably the juniper, while others were given several names. There are twenty names for thorns in the Bible. Also, much of the material of the Old Testament originated as songs or ballads and was handed down over the generations, probably resulting in changes in the words for the plants. Translators made errors as well. Scripture sometimes contained little description of the plants, so translators substituted plants found in their own lands for those found in Scripture. Editors added their own opinions, sometimes changing the meaning of the texts. Aspens were called mulberries and mulberries were sycamine; acanthus became nettle, dill was anise and the terebinth an elm.

Most of the plants mentioned in the Bible still grow in the Holy Land, and some also grow in other parts of the world with a Mediterranean climate. Fig, pomegranate and olive trees flourish in California, and palm trees grow in Florida, South America and Australia. Other species, including grapes and many of the herbs, vegetables and trees, grow in cooler climates.

PART TWO

Ancient Medicine and Healing

"On the banks, on both sides of the river, there will grow all kinds of trees for food....Their fruit will be for food, and their leaves for healing."
—*Ezekiel 47:12*

                  𝒫lants were the main source of remedies for healing in biblical times. People had observed wild animals munching on selected grasses and birds becoming inebriated after feeding on certain berries, and had experimented with plants to find calming and healing relief for weariness and pain.

Herbal medicines were used in ancient Egypt as far back as 10,000 B.C. and by the end of the fourth millennium B.C. the priest-physicians of Egypt had begun to systematize their traditions of healing. They may not have understood why a specific plant worked, but they had learned from experience that its use in treatment was beneficial.

Writing medical prescriptions was one of the first duties assigned to scribes of ancient Egypt, who recorded prescriptions on baked clay tablets, tombs of kings and pharaohs and a large number of medical papyri.

By the time of the Old Kingdom (2686–2181 B.C.), such disciplines as gynecology, surgery and veterinary medicine had developed. Physicians specialized in eye, head or stomach problems. Fiber splints for fractures from around 2800 B.C. have been found. Engraved depictions of surgery were found on a tomb near Memphis dating from around 2500 B.C. Paintings on the Physician's Tomb at Saqqara from 1500 B.C. show men manipulating the hands and feet of others. Temple carvings and reliefs describe the use of essential oils by priests and physicians.

Papyri probably date from the very early third millennium B.C. It is thought that parts of the medical papyri were written during this time, even though only copies from later periods have survived. Oldest of the existing texts is the Kahun papyrus dealing with female diseases and conception, from about 1825 B.C. The Edwin Smith papyrus, called the "Book of Wounds," appeared around 1550 B.C., but the text may have originated between 3000 and 2600 B.C.

The Ebers papyrus, also from about 1500 B.C., is the most comprehensive of the papyri, containing almost nine hundred prescriptions for laxatives, elimination of intestinal worms, stomach ailments, eye, heart and other conditions. This document, over 870 feet long, contains poetic language, comparing a boil with "wrinkled fruit" and unconsciousness with "fleeting breath." It recommends myrrh for wounds.

Texts from the Ramesseum temple library in Thebes include prescriptions to help pregnant women and their children, and papyri found in Deir el-Medina include incantations against headaches, called "half-head" as in the Greek word *hemikrania*, from which our word *migraine* comes.

The Assyrian Herbal, first published in 1924, incorporates information gleaned from 660 clay tablets found in the library of the palace of Ashurbanipal, an Assyrian king who ruled Nineveh from 668 to 626 B.C. The tablets contain medical texts thought to be of Babylonian origin from the period 2000–3000 B.C. The *Herbal* includes 250 names of plants, drugs and minerals used medicinally. Among the drugs of vegetable origin were almond oil, calendula, chamomile, fennel, myrrh, licorice, lupine, mandrake, opium poppy, pomegranate, saffron and turmeric.

Almonds, almond tree, Bible Garden,
Congregation B'nai Shalom, Walnut Creek, CA

Pomegranates, Neot Kedumim, Lod, Israel

Medicine in the Promised Land

The Israelites, who spent several hundred years in Egypt before coming to the Promised Land, knew Egyptian medical practices and brought this knowledge with them.

In earliest times, however, their priests taught that people should look to God for health and healing. Disease was seen as a punishment from God to be cured only by God. According to Deuteronomy 28:22: "The Lord will afflict you with consumption, fever, inflammation...." There were no physicians and people relied on herbal folk remedies, simple powders, ointments and salves for treatment. A legend developed that remedies were suppressed so that people would pray to God for mercy instead of depending on remedies for healing.

Priests became health officials as they enforced the law of Moses, which laid down high standards for hygiene. In the Pentateuch, the first five books of the Bible, ascribed to Moses, religious laws resulted in good hygiene. They governed diet and food preparation. Laws about unclean animals, purification of individuals, contact with the dead and the leprous were preventive in their effect. A thorough cleansing of households preceded great annual feasts. Observance of the Sabbath, with fasting and resting, was important for reducing stress. Liberal use of running water was both curative and preventive.

Leviticus 13 prescribes a quasi-medical role for the priests, who were to examine all kinds of skin afflictions, determine whether they were leprous or not and treat according to their findings.

Medical knowledge was slow to advance since the prophets were not considered healers, though their medical miracles were acknowledged and accepted. It was not until the Hellenistic period (332–152 B.C.) that the Jewish medical profession developed. In about 180 B.C. Sirach tells us:

> Honor physicians for their services, for the Lord created them; for their gift of healing comes from the Most High... (38:1–2)

> The Lord created medicines out of the earth, and the sensible will not despise them. Was not water made sweet with a tree in order that its power might be known?... By them the physician heals and takes away pain; the pharmacist makes a mixture from them. (38:4–8)

The Talmud, written during this time, identifies about seventy herbs and other plants as having medicinal properties, some for cures, others for prevention. The list includes olives, dates, pomegranates, garlic, hyssop, cumin and other plants used mainly for food. Leaves of *ara* (bay laurel) and *ezov* (hyssop) were recommended for intestinal worms and *shihlayim* (garden cress) for intestinal ailments. For *dema de-reisha,* "blood pressure in the head," *hadas* (myrtle) and *Rosa canina* (wild rose) were suggested. There were remedies for skin and liver ailments, hemorrhages, eye problems and scurvy.

Other writings tell us about the knowledge and use of plant remedies. In *The Book of Jubilees,* written in the first century B.C., we are told that the angels revealed many remedies to Noah, who recorded them in a book. Asaph the physician states that Noah, who had been taught about the remedies to be found in trees, plants and roots, wrote them in a book that he gave to his son Shem and was later used by physicians.

Flavius Josephus, first-century historian, wrote that the Jewish sect called the Essenes displayed "an extraordinary interest in the writing out of ancients, singling out...those which make for the welfare of the soul and body," and with the help of these texts, he investigated medicinal roots and the properties of stones.

Healing in Scripture

Balm, figs and oil are the only plant products mentioned in the Bible with reference to healing. In Jeremiah 8:22 the prophet cries: "Is there no balm in Gilead? / Is there no physician there?" Isaiah prescribes "a lump of figs" for King Hezekiah's boil (38:21) and speaks of "bruises and sores and bleeding wounds" that "have not been drained, or bound up, or softened with oil" (1:6).

Michael Zohary, Israeli biblical scholar, states that herbal remedies were numerous and specific in biblical times. They are not named in Scripture because mentioning the medicinal uses of plants would defy "the belief in God's exclusive healing power."

In the Old Testament most of the miracles of healing were the result of God reversing a plague or punishment, as in Numbers 16:46–48 when the plague was stopped after Aaron made atonement for the people. The healing of natural disease was rare and performed by the prophets. In 1 Kings 17:17–22 Elijah revives the son of the widow of Zarephath, and in 2 Kings 5:8–14 Elisha cures Naaman of his leprosy.

In the New Testament all cures are of natural diseases. The Gospels record at least thirty-five instances of Jesus healing individuals as well as groups of people. The first account of Jesus' healing is found in Matthew 4:23:

> Jesus went throughout Galilee, teaching in their synagogues and proclaiming the good news of the kingdom and curing every disease and every sickness among the people.

Jesus cleansed lepers, healed people who were blind, deaf, lame and epileptic, and cast out demons. He healed a woman with a hemorrhage, a man with a withered hand and a man with dropsy. He raised Lazarus from the dead.

The apostles healed many people, and Luke tells about many of these healings in the Acts of the Apostles. Acts tells about Peter healing the sick that were carried out into the streets "in order that Peter's shadow might fall on some of them" and those brought from the towns around Jerusalem, saying, "and they were all cured" (5:15–16). In Malta, Paul healed the father of Publius who was sick in bed with fever and dysentery (28:8).

Faith in Jesus and the kingdom of God seems to have been a condition of healing. The centurion's servant is healed because of his master's faith (Matthew 8:5–13). Some touched Jesus' person or garment and were healed.

The woman suffering from hemorrhages for twelve years touched the fringe of Jesus' cloak, saying to herself, "If I only touch his cloak, I will be made well." And Jesus said to her, "Take heart, daughter; your faith has made you well" (Matthew 9:20–22). In other cases Jesus' touch healed the person. After he touched Peter's mother-in-law "the fever left her" (Matthew 8:14–15).

Healing was more than physical. Jesus healed the whole person, often forgiving sin as a way of healing the body. James 5:15–16 says:

> The prayer of faith will save the sick, and the Lord will raise them up; and anyone who has committed sins will be forgiven. Therefore confess your sins to one another, and pray for one another, so that you may be healed.

Symbolism of Biblical Plants

Plants were often used as symbols in Scripture. The prophets of the Old Testament and Jesus in the New Testament all used trees, vines, fruit and herbs to represent God's goodness, his wrath and his mercy. Farmers and herders, who knew well the fruits of the vine, the fields and trees that provided sustenance for them and their livestock, understood the messages conveyed.

Thorns and prickly plants symbolized sin and its consequences. In the Garden of Eden, the Lord God tells Adam that the earth will bring forth

Our Lady's Thistle, Herb Garden, Niagara Parks
Botanical Gardens, Niagara Falls, Ontario, Canada

"thorns and thistles" because he listened to Eve and ate the apple (Genesis 3:17–18).

Prophets used the fig, olive and vine to express God's goodness in terms of a fertile land that yielded a bountiful crop. A rich harvest on earth was the reward of righteousness, and barren land and trees were the punishment for sinfulness. Abundance of the harvest proved God's love for man. Rapidly fading wild plants symbolized the transience of life: "The grass withers, the flower fades…" (Isaiah 40:8).

Jesus used the parable of the lilies of the field to illustrate the benefits of striving for the kingdom of God (Matthew 6:25–33). He compared the kingdom of God to the mustard seed, which when it "grows up...becomes the greatest of all shrubs" (Mark 4:30–32), and used the vine and the branch to represent the relationship between God and man.

The characteristics of plants made them suitable for use in various events and rituals in the Bible. Proud like the cedar, man was punished with leprosy, and once cured, he would be humble like the hyssop (Leviticus 14:2–4). Jesus, symbol of humility on the cross, was offered sour wine on a sponge hung on branches of hyssop, the symbol of humility in nature.

Stately palm trees were associated with rejoicing on the first day of the Feast of Tabernacles and during Jesus' triumphal entry into Jerusalem. Cedar branches, which remain unchanged through the seasons, represented constancy and virtue.

Palm trees, Neot Kedumim, Lod, Israel

The apple is the symbol of desire in the Jewish tradition, dipped in honey at Rosh Hashanah to symbolize the wish for a good, sweet New Year. It represents the fruit of knowledge in the Garden of Eden and the fall of man in the Christian tradition.

The white lily symbolizes purity and is associated with the Virgin Mary. The cyclamen, with its red center, symbolizes Mary's bleeding heart. The humble daisy represents the innocence of the Christ child.

PART THREE

Healing Plants and Their Histories

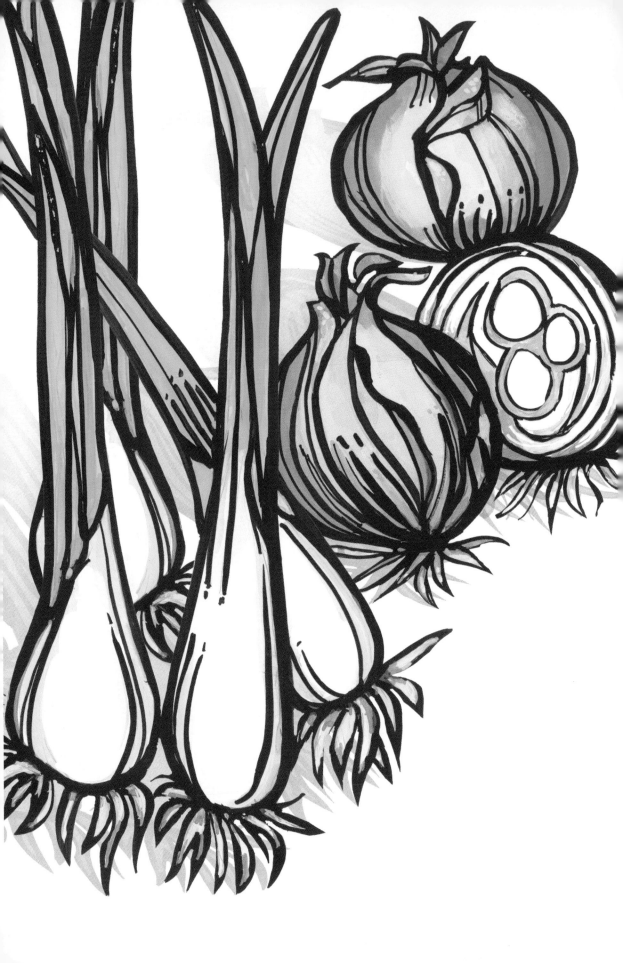

Alliums: The Flavoring Herbs

*"We remember the fish we used to eat in Egypt for nothing,
the cucumbers, the melons, the leeks, the onions, and the garlic...."*
—Numbers 11:5

The ancient Israelites had been shepherds and herdsmen with little opportunity to grow vegetables and herbs, so it was not until they were in Egypt that they learned to eat and savor leeks, onions and garlic, which had been cultivated there since 3000 B.C. They remembered the pungent alliums during their forty years of wandering in the desert when they tired of the manna God sent them: "There is nothing at all but this manna to look at" (Numbers 11:6). So, though the alliums are mentioned only once in the Bible, this reference emphasizes just how important this food was to the Israelites.

After they returned to Israel and settled in Canaan, farmers began to grow lentils, beans and other crops as well as the leeks, onions, garlic and cucumbers they had enjoyed in Egypt. The two-season climate of Israel—hot and dry, wet and cool—encouraged the development of bulbous-type plants.

Alliums can be considered herbs—plants valued for their medicinal, savory or aromatic qualities. They have all the healing powers associated with herbs and are prized for the zest they add to recipes. To the Egyptians, Romans and Israelites, the alliums' strong odors were not considered objectionable. Over the centuries leeks and onions have come to be seen not just as seasonings but also as separate foods.

Allium sativum

Garlic

Called the wonder drug of the herbal world, garlic was a symbol of strength and courage for the ancient Greeks and Romans. An Egyptian medical papyrus from around 1500 B.C. included more than two hundred prescriptions for garlic, recommending it for such problems as headaches, physical weakness and throat infections.

Romans knew of the Egyptians' high regard for garlic. The Roman author Pliny said divine honors were paid to the herb and that Egyptians considered it one of their deities. The Roman satirist Juvenal wrote of the ancient Egyptians' high esteem of onions and garlic:

> 'Tis mortal sin an onion to devour;
> Each clove of garlic hath a sacred power.

The builders of the great pyramid at Giza ate garlic to give them strength; the Romans gave it to their workmen for strength and their soldiers for courage in battle, and the Greek athletes at Olympic games chewed it to improve their chances of victory.

The Hebrews believed that garlic increased virility and relied on it to "be fruitful and multiply," as directed in Genesis. The Talmud directs that many kinds of food should be seasoned with garlic and lists the five properties of garlic, which was to be consumed on Shabbat (Friday):

It keeps the body warm.

It brightens the face.

It increases semen.

It kills parasites.

It fosters love and removes jealousy.

The Hebrew plural word *shumim* occurs only once in the Old Testament, and has been translated as "garlic." After the Israelites left Egypt, they remembered the garlic and onions and the other foods they enjoyed in Egypt. Tiring of the abundant manna they found in the desert, they complained to Moses, saying, "Surely it was better for us in Egypt" (Numbers 11:18). Their complaints brought down the wrath of God and the people who had the "strong craving" for the food of Egypt (11:4) were struck with the plague.

The Mishna, a collection of Jewish traditions found in the Talmud, records that the Israelites were so fond of garlic that they proudly called themselves "garlic eaters."

Depictions of garlic have been found on the walls of Egyptian tombs dating back to 3200 B.C. Remains of garlic were found in the Cave of the Pool at En-Gedi in Israel.

Hippocrates, fourth-century B.C. Greek physician, prescribed garlic as a treatment for uterine tumors and cancers. A natural antibiotic, garlic is used for infections of all kinds, parasites and fungi. It helps circulatory and intestinal problems and boosts the immune system. Its anti-inflammatory qualities counteract joint pain. Grated garlic and honey is recommended for coughs.

Garlic is often eaten raw on slices of bread in the Mediterranean region. Recipes using garlic include a garlic and lime dip made with mayonnaise, hot garlic sauce with mint and a garlic mint relish. Parsley, apple and anise seed are recommended to counteract the aftertaste. It is said that the garlic aroma dissipates after a brief soak in a hot bath.

The English name comes from the Anglo Saxon words *gar*, meaning "spear," and *lac*, meaning "plant." *Spear* may refer either to the shape of the leaves or the fact that garlic promotes warlike behavior.

Meditation

What has garlic got to do with God? What on earth in our contemporary world would make me thank God for garlic, especially ten agonizing minutes after eating it when my beloved wants a conversation! But oh, how fine the sauce that hides it!

In the shed are remnants of last year's garden. Side by side sit lily bulbs and a lonely garlic bulb, and I must wonder how the ancients discerned the healing enhancements of the one or of any growing thing. Did God reveal it somewhere, sometime? Or was it the daring, the bold and perhaps the hungry driven to try anything regardless of consequences? Or, gracious God, did you not rather provide wisdom to the seekers and observers, wisdom to the cooks and healers, to notice: Ah, this thing has made me well? I'll tell others and I'll praise the creator whose love provided it somehow in eons past. And in the end may I never forget,

> Therefore do not worry, saying, "What will we eat?"...our heavenly Father knows that you need all these things. But strive first for the kingdom of God and his righteousness, and all these things will be given to you as well. (Matthew 6:31–33)

Allium porrum

Leek

The Hebrew word *chatzir* occurs more than a dozen times in the Old Testament and has been translated variously as "grass," "herb" and "hay," depending on its context. The most ancient Greek translators used the word *prasa* (leeks) to represent the word *chatzir*. In Numbers 11:5 it has been translated as "leek," possibly because of its association with onions and because these vegetables were commonly used in Egypt at that time.

Some scholars consider fenugreek (*Trigonella foenum-graecum*), *hasir* in Hebrew, to be the leek mentioned in the Bible, while others point out that the fact that Israelis use the leek so abundantly today, rather than fenugreek, "is a potent argument against the latter plant, since Hebrews are recognized... for the tenacity and persistence of their customs through the ages."

The leek was held sacred in Egypt and was dedicated to or symbolic of a well-known deity. Pliny wrote that the first-century emperor Nero was so fond of leeks that he was referred to as *Porrophagus*, "the leek eater." Food of the poor, leeks were considered a symbol of humility.

Chrysoprasus, a Greek word meaning "golden leek," is named in Revelation 21:20 as the tenth precious jewel in the foundation in the wall of the heavenly city of Jerusalem. Like the leek, the stone has a pale green cast. In the sixth century the leek became the emblem of Wales after King Cadwallader's men, ordered by Saint David to wear leeks on their caps to distinguish them from the invading Saxons, repelled the Germanic hordes. Green and white are still the Welsh colors, even though the daffodil is now the national flower.

In biblical times a favorite dish was a porridge made from the white bulb of leeks, rice, crushed almonds and honey. Leeks and scallions (the name came from the city of Ashkelon) were rubbed with olive oil and grilled. In Egypt, it was said, the "inhabitants eat their leek and barley bread with avidity" (Balfour, *The Plants of the Bible*). Leeks are a major ingredient in the French soup vichyssoise and in the Scottish soup cock-a-leekie.

In *Banckes's Herbal* of 1525 we read that the juice of leeks should be taken for a cough and that a mixture of leeks and honey will heal a wound. Herbalist John Gerard prescribed leek broth for obesity, kidney complaints, intestinal disorders and coughs. If a child swallowed a pointed object such as a nail, boiled leeks eaten immediately would encase the sharp object and protect the stomach and bowel from perforation. More recently, the Cherokee people ate the leaves of wild leek (*Allium tricoccum*) to treat colds and croup and for a spring tonic. The warm juice of leaves and bulb applied to the ear soothed an earache.

An old English adage advises:

> Eate Leeks in Lide (March) and Ramsins in May
> And all the year after Physitians may play.

A modern herbal suggests a puree of cooked leeks sweetened with honey and taken a spoonful or two at a time, for colds, coughs and sore throats.

Leeks differ from garlic and onions in the shape of the leaf, which is broad, flat and more succulent than the hollow cylinder of the other alliums. Leeks can be grown in pots and tubs for their greenery, and the cook can clip the leaves for seasoning soups and salads. The bulbs can be harvested in the fall or left in the ground to be dug as needed.

Meditation

Then God said, "Let the earth put forth vegetation: plants yield-
ing seed, and fruit trees of every kind on earth that bear fruit
with the seed in it." And it was so...And God saw that it was
good. And there was evening and there was morning, the third
day. (Genesis 1:11–13)

O creation's abundance of green and vivid growth! Poets
and lovers wonder amazed; scholars and researchers compile
lists, identify, describe; historians search the centuries for clues,
connections, significance—no end, it seems, no end to the green
things growing—to feed us, heal us, delight us.

But what are they really, these green things yielding food
and seed and healing? They are revelation of a providing God!
No chance or accident, no whim of irrational power. God of
ours, you have created according to a marvelous master plan of
providing love. And all that you created is good, wondrously
good! You willed our wholeness and our health.

But you leave it up to me to unravel the secret of each good
thing. Like the pale green leek, sleek and smooth, food of the
poor and symbol of humility. Creator God, slow me down and
teach me the secrets of healing that you planned for me on
that third day and each day since.

Allium cepa

Onion

Considered so sacred that Egyptian priests were forbidden to eat them, onions were represented in many tomb paintings and even buried with royalty. They were found in the breasts of mummies. The odorous bulb represented the universe to the ancient Egyptians, who thought the spheres of heaven, earth and hell were concentric, like layers of onion.

Long cultivated in Egypt, onions date back six thousand years or more. They were regarded as a cure-all, prized for their aphrodisiac, antiseptic and digestive qualities and considered a necessity in the diets of workers building the pyramids. The Greek historian Herodotus wrote that Egyptian pharaohs spent nine tons of gold for onions to feed the slaves and laborers, many of them Israelites, who built the pyramids. An ancient inscription in the Great Pyramid of Cheops, built about 3700 B.C., states that sixteen hundred talents of silver (about $3,481,600) had been paid to provide the workers with onions, garlic and radishes.

The children of Israel, remembering the sweet soft Egyptian onions (*basal* in Hebrew), lusted after them in the desert and even longed to return to Egypt for them. Later they cultivated onions as well as garlic, and bulb scales of onions and bulbs of garlic were found in the Cave of the Treasure in Nahal Mishmar near the Dead Sea. The remains are said to be from the late Chalcolithic period or Early Bronze Age, sometime between 3820 and 2820 B.C.

The Hebrew plural word *betzalim* in Numbers 11:5 has been translated as "onions." The pungent bulbs became so much a part of the Israelite diet that an onion board, bread dough covered with sautéed onions and poppy seeds and baked, was traditionally served at the feast that followed the circumcision of a male infant. Honey and onion sandwiches were called the workingman's lunch.

To ward off the plague in medieval Europe bunches of onions were hung on the doors of homes and in places where people congregated. It was thought that the bulbs would draw to themselves the disease that might otherwise afflict the people. In England the onion was used as a weather oracle:

> Onion's skin is very thin,
> Mild winter coming in,
>
> Onion's skin thick and tough
> Coming winter cold and rough.
>
> —Addison, *The Illustrated Plant Lore*

Highly regarded by folk healers for centuries, onions are said to be a natural antibiotic. They are anti-inflammatory, helping edema, and antifungal, treating worms, warts and boils. Onions may prevent hair loss and protect against cancer. Syrup made of boiled or roasted onions and honey is recommended for coughs and colds.

Botanists claim there are more than five hundred species of onion, most edible and some ornamental. Sweet Spanish onions are said to be close kin to the large onions favored by the people of the Holy Land. The English word *onion* comes from the French *oignon*, and perhaps the best-known use for onions is in French onion soup.

Meditation

O imagination of a creator God, who made a smelly thing delight my taste—at first—and heal me. Stuff of pizzas and pastas, parties and bread sticks. Smile and savor, but later don't come too close.

Jesus, when you took residence in this created world, when you set up your dwelling as a tiny baby born of Mary the Virgin, and later when you were circumcised, were there celebrations? Did your mother, grandmother, relatives or neighbors make onion boards baked rich with poppy seeds and sautéed onions? And what other rituals were theirs, cherished of old, soon to find fulfillment in you, who were destined to be the ultimate healer? Will we ever fully know? Do we need to? I suppose it's enough to live the now fully!

So for now, right now, Gentle Healer, before all that dying and rising—yours and mine—let me celebrate with you the good things of this earth, ring after onion ring.

ALLIUMS: THE FLAVORING HERBS

The Balm of Gilead and Other Balms

"Bring balm for her wound;
perhaps she may be healed."
—Jeremiah 51:8

The Hebrew word for balm—*tzari, sori, tsori*—means "resin" or "gum" and refers to the fragrance of the plant. Though its source varies with the time and place, balm has been used from earliest times to heal and soothe man and his ailments. Archaeologists have found seeds of pistacia varieties dating as far back as 3500 B.C. and remains of *Balanites aegyptiaca* in Egypt from the Third Dynasty (2600 B.C.). Excavations at En-Gedi, on the western shore of the Dead Sea in Israel, unearthed tools, pottery and furnaces of ancient workshops for the production of balm and perfume. Experts agree that the first balm was originally a local plant and that later it was imported from southern Arabia.

In the Bible balm is first mentioned in Genesis, in the story of Joseph, son of Jacob, whose brothers having thrown him in a pit looked up and "saw a caravan of Ishmaelites coming from Gilead, with their camels carrying gum, balm, and resin, on their way to carry it down to Egypt" (Genesis 37:25). This is said to have occurred in 1727 B.C.

The healing properties of balm are well documented by Jeremiah. The prophet first mourns for his people who have turned away from God: "Is there no balm in Gilead? / Is there no physician there?" (Jeremiah 8:22).

Later he says,

> Go up to Gilead, and take balm,
>> O virgin daughter Egypt!
> In vain you have used many medicines;
>> there is no healing for you (Jeremiah 46:11).

And when the Lord destroys Babylon, the oracle suggests, "Bring balm for her wound; / perhaps she may be healed" (Jeremiah 51:8).

Balm was used in making perfume and was an ingredient in the holy oil used in the temple. Rabbi Shlomo ben Yitzhak, known as Rashi, the famous biblical and Talmudic commentator of the eleventh century, said that balm was the resin named as one of the ingredients of incense used in the tabernacle (Exodus 30:34).

Balm was an emblem of Palestine and a symbol of spiritual healing. After the Roman conquest, soldiers carried balm branches back to Rome as symbols of their victory over the Hebrews.

Balanites aegyptiaca
Jericho Balsam,
Balm of Mecca

Native to Egypt, *Balanites aegyptiaca* grew on the plains of Jericho and near the Dead Sea. It is the source of the balm mentioned in Genesis and Jeremiah. This is a desert-loving plant, a small, scrubby tree that still grows among the limestone hills of Palestine.

Jericho balsam also grows near the well at Materieh in Egypt, where tradition says that while the holy family rested there, Mary washed her infant Jesus in water drawn from the well. She threw the water on the ground, and wherever the water fell, balsam trees sprang up. The oil of these trees is said to have a sweeter fragrance and greater healing power than any other balsam. The grove of balsam was planted in the days of Cleopatra from seeds or young trees brought from Jericho.

The monks of Jericho consider this the biblical balm, preparing an oily gum from the fruit of the plant, which they sell to travelers as the Balm of Gilead.

Remains of the fruit, which was used as a laxative, were found in Egypt as early as 2600 B.C. In the third century, Theophrastus mentioned that Egyptian perfumers used the bruised husks of the fruit. The fruits were also pounded and boiled to extract medicinal oils that were poured over open wounds as an antiseptic. Balm was used as breath sweetener and medicinally as a stomach tonic and astringent. As a folk remedy it was used for burns, cough, herpes, colic, malaria, rheumatism and syphilis. One chronicler of folk uses called it False Balsam and wrote that *zaqqum* oil made from kernels of the ripe fruit was valued as a cure for all pains in bones or joints, whether from rheumatism or at the onset of fever, and was rubbed in at night after a bath.

Axes, writing boards, walking sticks and wooden bowls were made from the wood of the shrub, and the spiny branches were used to corral animals.

Meditation

Lord, you went to Jericho on the west side of the Jordan. It is desert there, hot, not far from the Dead Sea. You talked, taught and cured there. Did you walk among the limestone hills, break a branch of the scrubby little balsam, rub it between your fingers, feel its stickiness, enjoy its fragrance?

Which words in Jericho healed best? Mark and Luke tell how you healed blind Bartimaeus outside town. Jericho is the place of the little man Zacchaeus who dined with you, and Jericho, too, is the setting for the account of the Good Samaritan.

Lord, when the healing and teaching and dining were finished, did you sit among the little desert balsam trees, rub a tiny ball of gum and think, perhaps, of wounds coming, wounds in need of balm? Lord, what were your thoughts among the desert hills in the darkness of the desert night? How I wish I could sit there with you and know that fragrance.

Commiphora opobalsamum
Balsam of Gilead

Balquis, the Queen of Sheba who came to test the fame of Solomon in 995 B.C., was so astounded at his great wisdom, accomplishments and riches that she gave him "one hundred twenty talents of gold, a great quantity of spices, and precious stones" (1 Kings 10:10). Balm was included in the spices and King Solomon, impressed by the "virtues" of the balm that Balquis brought him, persuaded her to send him young trees or seeds of balsam, which he planted on the Plain of Jericho.

The gardens were twenty to thirty miles from Gilead, in more favorable soil and climate. The groves of balsam trees became one of the treasures of the country and were described by Theophrastus in 300 B.C. They survived the destruction of Judea but disappeared in the seventh century, when the Muslims conquered Palestine.

The balsam of Gilead is a small, stiff-branched evergreen tree, seldom more than fifteen feet tall, with straggling branches and scanty trifoliate leaves. White flowers appear in clusters of three at the same time as the leaves. The balm is a fragrant resin or gum obtained either by making incisions in the stem and branches or from the fruit, which can be green or ripe.

This balm was an ingredient of the holy oil for the Temple and was used in perfumes. It was a healing agent for wounds and an antidote for snakebites.

Meditation

Lord, do you smile at us when we plant trees? Perhaps we will be long gone before the trees mature and become useful.

A queen's gift long ago inspired a wise man to plant trees that became a nation's treasure for centuries. They say the resin from these trees served in liturgical rituals and healing. What do you think, Lord? Are there Solomons today wise enough to recognize true treasures and selfless enough to know that shade and fruits are for generations beyond?

In our household a ninety-two-year-old planted a young shade tree from her little bit of pocket money. At ninety-eight she's still alive and observing her tree. Lord, will she have a chance to enjoy her shade, both here and there?

Pistacia lentiscus
Lentisk or Mastic Tree

Some biblical botanists regard the Hebrew word *tzori, tzeri* or *tzari* as referring either to the gum of *Balanites aegyptiaca* or of *Pistacia lentiscus*. Both were
common in Palestine, and the latter, native to Palestine, was abundant in the
rocky country of Gilead.

The mastic tree *Pistacia lenticus* is mentioned only once, in the apocalyp-
tic writing of the story of Susanna, but a marginal reading for the balm of
Genesis 37:25 is *mastic*, which suggests the shrub *Pistacia lentiscus*. Described
as a bushy evergreen, the desert-loving mastic tree grows to ten or fifteen feet
in height. Aromatic balm, or *tzori*, extracted from the tree was chewed to sweet-
en the breath and strengthen and massage the gums. In the ancient world the
balm was renowned as a powerful therapeutic agent and was the basis of aromatic and astringent preparations.

The balm in Genesis 43:11 "...take in your bags...a little balm and a little
honey" is thought to be the product of the lentisk or mastic tree. Carbonized
seeds of *Pistacia* varieties dating to the Middle Stone Age period have been
found in archeological sites.

Meditation

The story of Susanna—legend or life? Her story tells the human truth of lust, injustice and rage vindicated in a court case that would probably hold today. But the story brings another memory, a very personal one, which surely delighted you, Lord!

Surely you remember a certain 6 a.m. Mass long ago, served by a lovely, innocent ten-year-old boy? What an incredible thing for him to trudge that far to Mass at that early hour in the Lenten dark! I admired the child. That morning the pastor began, "There was a man living in Babylon whose name was Joakim. He married the daughter of Hilkiah, named Susanna, a very beautiful woman and one who feared the Lord. Her parents were righteous, and had trained their daughter according to the law of Moses. Joakim was very rich, and had a fine garden adjoining his house..." (Daniel 13:1–4). Suddenly the pastor stopped, looked at the sleepy boy then at his little congregation: "Enough for today; you know about the trees in that garden."

Bitter Herbs

"They shall eat the lamb that same night;
they shall eat it roasted over the fire
with unleavened bread and bitter herbs."
—*Exodus 12:8*

$\mathcal{E}$xodus tells us that the Lord commanded the Israelites to eat the lamb with unleavened bread and bitter herbs, on what was to be their last night in Egypt. For that night the Lord struck down all of the firstborn in Egypt, except those whose houses had been marked with the blood of the lamb. When the cruel pharaoh, who had refused to let the Israelites go, realized what had happened, he drove the Hebrews out of Egypt, ending 430 years of slavery.

Passover, or Pesach, commemorating the destroying angel passing over the houses of the Israelites, is a celebration of the Jews' deliverance from Egypt. It is the oldest of Jewish festivals, observed in ancient times by nomadic shepherds to usher in the spring season.

Biblical commentator Aben Ezra said the Jews always ate bitter herbs, called *maror* or *merorim*, with their food, a custom they may have learned from the Egyptians. The greens grew wild and were easily obtained. Ancient Egyptians placed bowls of various greens, mixed with mustard, on the table and dipped their bread into the mixture while eating.

Rabbinic tradition tells that the number of bitter herbs should be five, with three of them being lettuce, endive and chicory. Some biblical commentators believe that the bitter herbs included dandelion and sorrel and that endive was not yet known in Egypt or Palestine. It is thought that watercress was also used. Later the Samaritans included *murrar*, the yellow star thistle, and some Europeans substituted horseradish or parsley for "bitter herbs."

During the Seder meal of Passover, a bundle of bitter herbs is placed on the table to represent the bitterness experienced by the slaves in Egypt.

Cichorium intybus

Chicory

Chicory was well known to the ancient Egyptians, Greeks and Romans, who considered it a health food and used the plant for culinary and medicinal purposes. The Israelites added symbolic meaning associated with bitterness.

Leaves were served whole or shredded in salads with vinegar and oil, their bitterness reminding them of their enslavement in Egypt. The heart of the plant, which lost its bitterness when blanched or par-boiled, was served as a vegetable, the sweetness symbolizing the joy of deliverance. The flowers were eaten fresh or pickled in salads, and the roots were used as a coffee substitute and as an antidote to poison.

The botanical name *Cichorium* comes from the Greek word *kichore*, meaning "salad" or "root vegetable." In Palestine it was called *Elik* or *Elitsh*. The English called it *succory*.

Pliny, first-century Roman author, mentions wild chicory and the cultivated variety, both grown in Egypt, and said that the juice used with rose oil and vinegar relieved headaches; mixed with wine it helped liver and bladder conditions. Prospero Alpini, sixteenth-century Egyptologist, said chicory was considered a cooling herb, used to treat feverish diseases, both internally and externally.

Chicory was used as a diuretic and a laxative, the bitter taste stimulating digestion. It was known as "liver's friend" and had a folk reputation as a cure or preventive of liver problems. Poultices of the leaves and flowers wrapped in a cloth were used for inflammations and skin lacerations.

Other uses for healing include the Bach flower remedy, which promotes selfless love, the flower essence to help create a more secure feeling in insecure persons and homeopathic prescribing for persons with sluggish digestion and over-relaxed bowels.

The bright blue flowers have been used by country folk to tell the time, and Linnaeus, famous Swedish botanist, used them in his horologe, or "floral clock" in his garden in Uppsala. In Sweden the blossoms open at 5:00 A.M. and close at 10:00 A.M. They open at 8:30 A.M. and close four hours later in the eastern part of the United States.

Dwarf chicory *(Cichorium pumilum),* one of the nine species of *Cichorium*, now grows in Israel. Chicory grows wild on roadsides and uncultivated fields.

Meditation

Bright flower, fragile, wild and available, herald of morning, hope of times to come. Summer nuisance in my backyard, grows everywhere wanted and unwanted. But wait. Stop. Reflect. Weed that zests a Passover lamb, root that becomes a poor cook's coffee, bitterness to remember bitterness's hope of freedom— then and now, for remembrances Hebrew and Christian.

Blue flower of the wayside, when you open to greet our fresh new mornings, do we remember the story of the Passover mysteries? Or will we uproot you from our hedges and cement you to nonexistence in our cities because we have forgotten?

Father, I hold in my hand the fragile flower and fragrant green of your chicory—wild and available—at least for now.

Taraxacum officinale
Dandelion

Used as a medicine in ancient Greece, where it originated, and praised in herbals of the Middle Ages, the tenacious plant was readily found in Egypt and the Holy Land. The genus name *Taraxacum* comes from the Greek words *taraxo*, meaning "disorder" and *takos*, meaning "remedy." The name is also a corruption of a Persian word for "bitter potherb" and an Arabian word meaning "edible."

As its many names suggest, the plant was well known in many countries. Gerard, sixteenth-century English herbalist, wrote of "*dens lionis*, the herb which is commonly called Dandelion" and "sends forth from the root long leaves deeply cut and gashed in the edges...." The flower, sweet in smell, he said, "is turned into a round downy blowbal that is carried away with the wind." Children used the flowers to tell time, blowing away at the seed heads, the number of puffs needed to blow them all away marking the hour.

The French called the herb *dent de lion* and the Germans *Löwenzahn* because its leaves resembled the jagged teeth of a lion. They likened the golden flowers to the tawny color of the royal animal's coat. The French also called it *pissenlit* because it was such a successful diuretic.

A century ago the townsfolk of Artas, a village in Palestine, called it *Salata el Ruhban* or Monk's Salad. They used the leaves and salads and made dandelion tea and dandelion wine, both considered excellent blood builders and spring tonics. The English called the plant Devil's Milk Pail because of the milky juice in its leaves and stems. They also called the flower Priest's Crown, thinking it resembled a medieval priest's shaved head after the seeds blew away.

Dandelions were among the herbs used by the Egyptians as table greens, and the Israelites learned to eat the bitter greens from them. Raw in salads, blanched or cooked with salt pork, the leaves were a bountiful vegetable. The roots were pickled or ground for dandelion coffee or mixed with coffee and the flowers used to make wine.

Tea made from fresh roots is used for liver, gall bladder and kidney ailments. The bitter taste stimulates the appetite, increases digestive tract activity and cleanses the blood and liver, helping rheumatism, gout and joint problems.

Folk remedies include use as a laxative and for rheumatism and sciatica. An apple and dandelion salad, with olive oil, lemon juice and basil leaves, is recommended for constipation. The leaves and flowers are rich in vitamins A and C and lecithin. Strained liquid from flowers simmered in water makes a cleansing wash for the skin or can be added to bathwater.

The flower essence helps balance energy, activity and enthusiasm for persons who are doing rather than being, finding little time for spiritual or emotional pursuits. In homeopathic medicine *Taraxacum* is prescribed for liver and digestive problems.

Meditation

Tenacious! Tough carpet of springtime gold, fresh and tender greens for a northern Easter's springtime Passover salad. My family gave up fighting them; we picked their soft gold blossoms for homemade wine, indeed a bitter, zestful wine! And who of us didn't make chains, link upon link, with white milk turning black on our hands and lasting days under our fingernails—to Mom's dismay.

Interesting, Lord, that the dandelion is a healer, a purifier of blood. Reminds me of the blood of the lamb outpoured. Such blood! Young, strong, pure healing blood—blood given; your blood, Lord, the warm blood of life and where it falls ever new life, ever fuller growth—like the persistent dandelion—tenacious, victorious.

Rumex acetosella

Sorrel

Biblical commentators believe that the bitter herbs of Scripture included sorrel, eaten as a salad. The weedy plant was common in Egypt and western Asia and would have been known to the Hebrews during the time of Moses, who led them out of Egypt.

The Latin name refers to the sour taste of the plant, which is commonly known as sour dock, sour suds and sour grass. It is also called sheep sorrel.

Two species of sorrel were common in Palestine early in the last century. *Rumex vesicarius*, called *hummeid*, was said to be deliciously acid and as good as French garden sorrel when young. The Muslim fellahin used it for stuffing in meat pastry, putting it inside the dough with meat and onions and baking it. For fasting food, *sumi*, the sorrel was used alone in the dough. The Arabs preferred *Rumex lacerus*, which they called *humsis*, finding the sour taste a pleasant change from the sweet dates they subsisted on, and fed it to their goats.

Rumex cyprius Murb. is the species that grows in Israel today, its spikes of flowers forming red borders along the roadsides in the desert in the early part of the year. The stems and leaves are used for making preserves.

In folk use sorrel leaf tea is used for fevers and inflammation and the root tea for diarrhea. Sorrel juice is diuretic; mixed with vinegar it treats skin infections. Sorrel is high in oxalic acid, and large doses may cause poisoning.

Native Americans used the lemon-flavored, vitamin-rich greens and flowers as a liver tonic and cleansing herb in the spring. Sorrel was an ingredient in an anticancer remedy known as *essiac*.

Small amounts are used in cooking. The leaves, chopped finely and mixed with vinegar and sugar, make a green sauce. They can be added to soups, salads and omelets. They act as a tenderizer when wrapped around meat.

The essence of *Rumex crispus* is used homeopathically for coughs, hoarseness, sore throats and some skin conditions.

Meditation

Its bitterness can heal and can poison. Lord, who would want to risk handling it if you don't know the measure! Beauty can heal, beauty can hurt. So can love.

A bitter herb—like beauty, like love—can taste of deliverance and freedom in the paschal hour. That same bitterness—like beauty, like love—can cause death when used beyond its gifted purpose. Ah, Lord, as ever, your mysterious ways allow both life and death—freedom's choice side by side. Would you teach me to know the difference? When does my love heal, and when is it a troublesome invader ruining every paschal supper?

Nasturtium officinale
Watercress

Used as a side dish at the Passover feast and other banquets, watercress was one of the bitter herbs but also symbolized eternal life and the coming of spring.

Writers about biblical plants seem to use the terms *watercress* and *garden cress (Lepidum sativum)* interchangeably, although they refer to different plants. Watercress is a juicy, vivid green plant growing in shallow creeks and ditches and along the edges of rivers and ponds. In the Holy Land it grows wild along the banks of streams and rivers. Garden cress is described as a tall herb with white flowers that grows wild but is cultivated in Egypt today for use as a stimulant and diuretic as well as in poultices. Later, the English botanist Gerard speaks of Indian cresses and "wilde water-Cresses." *Nasturtium aquatum minus* was "lesser water-Cresse."

Watercress was among the plants listed in Babylonian records and ancient seeds were found in Greece and in the tomb of Kha near Thebes in Egypt. The Greeks thought watercress's special properties helped with brain disorders and admonished the witless to "eat cress and get wit." Mixed with vinegar and placed on the forehead, this herb was said to revive those who felt "dull and drowsy."

A recipe for Sumerian watercress suggests one bundle for each serving, boiled a few minutes, cooled and pressed to remove water, then served with dressing as an accompaniment for meat or fish.

The Talmud recommends garden cress in remedies for intestinal ailments and for stopping hemorrhages. Alpini mentions cress seeds as one of several ingredients in a mixture of herbs and spices with honey that was deemed beneficial for the mind and body in general.

Watercress, with its pungent leaves and young stems, was said to stimulate the appetite and was used widely in salads, as a meat garnish and in biscuits. It was considered a blood cleanser and detoxifying herb for kidney ailments. The bruised leaves were used to treat blemishes and blotches on the face.

Called *stune* or *stime* in Anglo-Saxon, watercress was one of the nine sacred herbs used for healing. A healing charm for *stune* from a manuscript written about A.D. 1000 includes the following:

> Stune is this herb named, on stone hath she grown.
> She standeth again venom, pain she assaulteth.
> She is strong against those loathsome things that fare
>   throughout the land.

Meditation

Took a walk in my sister's creek and searched among the stones where soft fronds sway beneath the surface. Touched the wet greens as the clear water cooled and soothed. Remembered the blessing of the water at Easter Vigil, "At the very dawn of creation your Spirit breathed on the waters, making them the wellspring of all holiness." Yes, Lord, if only this humble creature could cleanse me once and for all!

Thought of the new earth covered with water; the Red Sea barrier to freedom, crossed over dry shod; the Jordan and John where water prepared the way for the paschal reality. Remembered another saying: "Since the beginning of the world, water, so humble and wonderful a creature, has been the source of life and fruitfulness" (Catechism of the Catholic Church 1218). Walked farther down the creek and continued to gather this bitter herb washed clean in mountain waters. So I could not help but think of you, Lord, when the water and the blood flowed from your side.

Yes, Lord, the watercress's soft green wetness reminds me of rivers of the past mingled with my own waters of decision— every day.

Cleansing Herbs

"Purge me with hyssop, and I shall be clean;
wash me, and I shall be whiter than snow."
—Psalm 51:7

Both the Old and New Testaments contain references to cleansing, from secret faults and idols, from filthiness of the body and disease, and from sin. Ceremonial purification according to Mosaic law is mentioned in connection with the Passover, cleansing of lepers, people and houses and the slaughter of the red heifer.

Hyssop, used in many of the cleansing rituals, was considered a purifying herb, literally as well as symbolically. It may have functioned as a deodorant, and its medicinal use was well known in biblical times. In the first century Pliny noted that the plant claimed cleansing properties in antiquity.

Nettles and thistles, used medicinally for cleansing and detoxifying the body, are used in the Bible to represent waste and desolation. The unwanted plants grew up in wheat fields and cow pastures as a reminder of God's punishment for man's original sin and later for Israel's breaking the covenant (Genesis 3:18; Hosea 9:6; 10:8).

Origanum maru, Majorana syriaca

Hyssop, Syrian Marjoram

"'Take a bunch of hyssop,
dip it in the blood that is in the basin,
and touch the lintel and the two doorposts
with the blood in the basin.'"

—Exodus 12:22

At least eighteen plants have been considered for the hyssop of the Bible, but modern botanists have identified *Origanum maru* or *Majorana syriaca* as the *ezov* of Scripture.

Many species are native to the region, and an Egyptian variety (*Origanum aegyptiaca*) grew in Egypt. *Majorana syriaca* is abundant in Israel and the Sinai desert among dwarf shrubbery, usually on stony ground.

The authors of *From Cedar to Hyssop* state, "Every Palestinian knows *Za'tar,* the little gray-green marjoram (*Origanum maru*) with the fragrant smell and masses of tiny white flowers, growing so commonly on rocks and terrace walls." They write that the strongest argument in favor of *Za'tar* is the fact that the Samaritans in their Passover ritual use it. "These rigid Conservatives may well be still using the same plant they have used for the last 2,000 years or so."

In the spring, around the time of Passover and Easter, hyssop displays the tiny flowers and thick, fuzzy leaves that, assembled in a bunch, will hold water and make an excellent sprinkler. This hyssop could serve as the paintbrush used on the eve of the Exodus and in the Passover ritual or the sponge offered Jesus on the Cross. "So they put a sponge full of the wine on a branch of hyssop and held it to his mouth" (John 19:29).

Hyssop was considered a sign of purification and might also have been used to sprinkle the people on Calvary to protect them from defilement on the eve of the Sabbath, since they were in the field of execution.

A bunch of hyssop was used to sprinkle the blood of the first paschal lamb and to sprinkle the altar and the people at the time of sacrifice. Together with cedar, hyssop was cast into the fire during the burning of the red heifer, and the ashes mingled with water formed the water of purification sprinkled over those who were unclean (Numbers 19:6, 18).

The Midrash Hagadol states, "You were proud like the cedar and the Holy One, Blessed be He, humbled you like this hyssop that is crushed by all."

Cedar and hyssop, representing pride and humility, were used in the ritual cleansing of lepers and houses (Leviticus 14:4–7, 49–52): "the priest shall command that two living clean birds and cedarwood and crimson yarn and hyssop be brought for the one who is to be cleansed" (14:4). The lowly hyssop was the symbol of humility in nature, just as Jesus on the Cross was considered the symbol of humility.

Dioscorides, Greek physician of the first century, referred to hyssop as the "holy herb." The Greeks called it "joy of the mountains," from the words *oros*, meaning "mountain" and *ganos*, meaning "joy." Greeks and Romans prized the aroma of the herb, and bridal couples wore crowns of woven marjoram. The Roman historian Pliny said the pulverized leaves were used as a dusting powder for skin eruptions and swelling.

Hyssop was one of the "strewing herbs" of the Middle Ages. Made into nosegays and bouquets, it was used to mask odors and ward off disease. Two illuminated medieval health handbooks of the late 1300s, the *Tacuinum* of Paris and *The Theatrum of the Casanatense Library,* Rome, included "Sweet Marjoram, *Maiorana*, the kind with a stronger aromatic power; good for the stomach, the brain, all the intestines."

In the last century in Palestine, *Origanum maru* was valued as a stimulant to the brain. Students ate it to clear their heads while studying, and orators used it to promote fluency. "He who eats *Zatar* his tongue shall not stammer" (Crowfoot, *From Cedar to Hyssop*).

The leaves are used in cooking and baking and as a popular spice eaten with bread and olive oil. In Lebanon children with colds or colic are given hyssop tea. The herb is said to help inflammation, degenerative arthritis and the aging process.

The caper plant (*Capparis aegyptiaca, C. spinosa*), which also grows on stony ground and is found growing between the massive stones of the Western Wall in Jerusalem, was once thought to be the biblical hyssop. Its branches could furnish a stick long enough to support the sponge offered Jesus on the cross. It is now considered the "desire" ("and desire fails") mentioned in Ecclesiastes 12:5. The ancient Israelis served capers as an appetizer, naming the flower buds "desire fails" because eating them assuaged hunger until the main course was ready.

Meditation

Hyssop, Lord! Its very mention makes me shudder. It wakens memories of your incredible suffering. You were dying, Lord, and so thirsty. I am a spectator, powerless, aching—would rather turn away.

Scripture says they used a hyssop branch to quench your thirst. Were they with you, against you or neither? But at least they were not passive! Did they give you common wine or vinegar or something mixed with gall? Translators do not agree. Are these the same, or does it really matter? Writings abound in meditation on your thirst and its bitter relief.

For me, today, Lord, I'm thinking about the humble hyssop with its tiny flowers and fuzzy leaves as it touched your lips. Had I been one of the Marys standing there, would I have tucked the blood-stained hyssop beneath my garments to press against my heart—to treasure this dying, growing thing and hold on to something of you?

CLEANSING HERBS

Urtica urens, U. dioica, U. pilulifera
Nettle, Small Nettle, Stinging Nettle, Roman Nettle

"Thorns shall grow over its strongholds,
nettles and thistles in its fortresses..."
—Isaiah 34:13

Biblical botanists point out that several Hebrew words in the Bible have all been translated as "nettle." The scientists agree that the words *kimosh* and *kimshon*, which mean "a prickly plant" and "ruin or destruction," are the nettles referred to in Isaiah and Hosea. This is the stinging nettle, several species of which exist in Palestine. They quickly invade land no longer cultivated. The Roman nettle is usually found among ruins, and the small nettle, in more open habitats, such as neglected gardens and fields.

The stinging nettle seems an apt symbol for the retribution God meted out to those who failed to keep his covenant. Its luxuriant growth makes desolate places uninhabitable, and the microscopic hairs on the leaves prick the skin of anyone touching them, injecting an irritating inflammatory acid. The Latin name for the genus, *Urtica*, means "to burn."

The Assyrians, however, valued the plant for its healing qualities. Their medical texts indicate it was used for coughs, eye ailments, scorpion bites and swellings and other conditions. Dioscorides suggested fresh chopped leaves be used as a plaster for septic wounds and the juice for nosebleeds.

Caesar's soldiers, unprepared for the damp cold in England, are said to have scoured their legs with stinging *Urtica pilulifera* to warm them. An ancient prescription, thought to date from the Roman occupation, reads: "Take nettles, and seethe them in oil, smear and rub all the body therewith; the cold will depart away."

In Judea nettles were considered a potherb, the leaves used as seasoning or cooked as a vegetable. In dairy country nettle leaves were preferred for curdling milk since they did not leave a bad taste. Country folk cooked nettle leaves in a stew and served it to cure almost any ailment.

Louise Baldensperger, who, in the early twentieth century, gathered lore about folk use of plants in Palestine, found that "People whip themselves with nettles for rheumatism, a most heroic remedy, rather like allowing oneself to be stung by bees for a cure."

In Europe nettle leaf tea is used as a blood purifier for gout and rheumatism. The high iron content makes it a good blood builder for anemic conditions. In homeopathic medicine *Urtica urens* treats bites and stings and other skin conditions with stinging, itching and burning.

Young nettle tops, cooked like spinach, are still used as a spring vegetable and tonic and nettle tea is considered a standby emergency medicine for plants. The tiny flowers are green.

Some writers believe acanthus (*Acanthus syriacus*) to be the biblical nettle. The leaves of this plant have served as models for leaf and scroll decorations since ancient times. Callimacus, Greek architect of the fifth century B.C., used the foliage pattern at the top of Corinthian columns. This plant is thought to be the nettles referred to in Zephaniah 2:9:

> Therefore as I live, says the LORD of hosts,
>   the God of Israel,
> Moab shall become like Sodom
>   and the Ammonites like Gomorrah,
> a land possessed by nettles and salt pits,
>   and a waste forever.

Acanthus has yellowish white flowers and is used as a diuretic and for digestive upsets.

Charul, which means "a rough, dry stick" in Hebrew, is the word used in Proverbs 24:30–31, and is thought to refer to *Sinapis arvensis* (charlock), a form of mustard:

> I passed by the field of one who was lazy,
>> by the vineyard of a stupid person;
> and see, it was all overgrown with thorns;
>> the ground was covered with nettles…

Also called field mustard, this plant, with large yellow flowers, was used in an old folk remedy for throat tumors. The seeds make a good substitute for mustard.

Meditation

Lord, my neighbor was ill last summer. I walked by her yard yesterday. Everything seemed so neglected. How could those stinging nettles on the back hedge take over so quickly? Who would buy her place now?

You know I'm restless, Lord. But I have my own responsibilities! Yes, I see her out there in her nettles—so fragile. She wants to get the place in shape before... Besides that, Lord, she's proud. Perhaps I'll stop by to pick nettle tips for tea. Silly, maybe, but I heard it cleanses spring fever. Perhaps we'll bridge the silence. Perhaps you'll be with us.

"Death has been swallowed up in victory."
"Where, O death, is your victory?

   Where, O death, is your sting?" (1 Corinthians 15:54–55)

CLEANSING HERBS

Silybum marianum
Milk Thistle
Also known as Holy Thistle,
Our Lady's Thistle

"You will know them by their fruits.
Are grapes gathered from thorns,
or figs from thistles?"
—Matthew 7:16

Thistles, thorns and nettles figure greatly throughout the Bible, providing vivid examples of the results of God's judgment on his people. When God cursed the earth for man's sin, he said to Adam, "[T]horns and thistles it shall bring forth for you" (Genesis 3:18).

In announcing judgment on Israel, the prophet says,

> The high places of Aven, the sin of Israel,
>   shall be destroyed.
> Thorn and thistle shall grow up on their altars. (Hosea 10:8)

It would seem that God's judgment and the prophecies have been fulfilled: 125 kinds of thistles now grow in the Holy Land. Hasselquist, the Swedish naturalist who explored the Holy Land in the mid-eighteenth century, noticed eight or ten varieties of thistle on the road between Jerusalem and Ramah, a distance of about five miles, and one on Mount Tabor. In the nineteenth century Clarke was amazed to find the earth between Nazareth and Tiberius covered with immense tracts of thistles, and Carruthers wrote, "thistles of gigantic size, overtopping the horse and his rider, abound in the rich plains of Gennesaret, Sharon, Esdraelon, and Jericho."

Thistles create the desolation with which they are associated in the Bible. The downy tufts attached to the fruit scatter the seeds widely, resulting in a profusion of plants that choke all other vegetation.

The Hebrew word *dardar* has been translated as "thistle." Milk thistle, common in Samaria and parts of Israel today, was called *khurfesh* in Palestine a century ago. The plant is easily recognized because of the white veins on its leaves, which give it the English name milk thistle. Tradition is that a drop of the Virgin's milk fell on the leaves and marked them for all time, when she stopped along the road to feed the infant Jesus, thus the names holy thistle, Our Lady's thistle and the Latin *marianum*.

In the first century Pliny wrote that consuming milk thistle carried off bile, and Dioscorides said the "leaves and roots are a remedy for those that have their bodies drawne backwards." Thistle has been used as a remedy for depression and liver problems in Europe for hundreds of years, and in Western herbal medicine thistle is used to protect and treat the liver. The plant contains anti-inflammatory agents helpful in relieving skin infections and disorders.

The young leaves are used in salads, and the heads were once eaten like artichokes. The Bedouins grind the seeds for food, and the seeds have served as coffee substitutes. Tea from the whole plant is said to improve the appetite and digestion and restore liver function.

Among other thistles, *Centaurea iberica* (Iberian centaury) is the species most commonly found in Palestine. The plant is distinguished from other this-tles by its whorled leaves and is called *dardur*, meaning "whorls," by the Arabs. The leaves lie flat on the ground throughout the winter. *Centaurea aegyptiaca*, a rare species, grows in the desert areas of the Negev and the Dead Sea region.

Golden thistle (*Scolyumus maculatus*) which grows in grain fields and in the lower altitudes of Israel, may be the "thorns" Matthew speaks of in 13:7.

Meditation

*"As for what fell among the thorns, these are the ones who hear;
but as they go on their way, they are choked by the cares and
riches and pleasures of life, and their fruit does not mature."
(Luke 8:14)*

*There are thistles growing at the edge of our field. Quite
pretty with their purple crowns. Formidable in their rooted-
ness. I tried to pick some for a vase. It was a waste of time and
added pricked fingers to my petty crosses.*

*Lord, thistle helps depression, they say. Lord, when you
walked the Galilean hills, surely there were thistles and
thorns on the roadside. Did your garments snag when the
wind drew them there? And did you know how easily we are
snagged by the cares and delights of our daily life? Take them,
Lord, and cleanse me of these depressions one after the other.*

Fruits of the Field

"For the LORD *your God is bringing you into a good land...*
a land of wheat and barley,
of vines and fig trees and pomegranates,
a land of olive trees and honey...."

—Deuteronomy 8:7–8

Fruits were a favorite and important part of the diet of the Israelites in biblical times. Fruits were refreshing, nourishing and beneficial for healing common ailments. God promised the Jews a fruitful land after they left Egypt, and the seven species mentioned in Deuteronomy flourished in the promised land of Canaan.

Referred to as "trees of the field" to distinguish them from the trees of the forest, fruit trees were so greatly valued that the Mosaic law forbade the destruction of any fruit tree, even in wartime. Only those that did not produce food could be cut.

"The choicest of the first fruits" were brought into the temple to honor God (Exodus 23:19), and fruits were part of the ritual in festivals. Sukkoth, the Feast of Tabernacles, celebrated the harvesting of grapes and other fruits and crops. The streets were decorated with palm leaves, green branches and fruit. *Haroset*, the dipping sauce used during Passover, was made from dates, figs, raisins and vinegar. During the Last Supper Jesus identified his betrayer as the "one who is dipping bread into the bowl with me" (Mark 14:20).

A story in the Talmud tells that fruit trees are planted for the future. An old man, planting a carob tree, is asked by a passerby why he plants it since it will not bear fruit for seventy years. "Just as I found the world full of carob trees that my grandparents before me planted for me, I am planting for my grandchildren after me," he says.

Malus sylvestris
Apple

"Sustain me with raisins
refresh me with apples;
for I am faint with love."
—*Song of Solomon 2:5*

"The tree of the knowledge of good and evil" (Genesis 2:9, 17) in the Garden of Eden may or may not have been an apple tree. Botanists and biblical scholars are divided about this and whether the word *apple* in the Bible refers to apples as we know them or to apricots, citron or even quince.

That the apple was a prized fruit is evident from references in Proverbs, Song of Solomon and Deuteronomy 32:10: "cared for him, guarded him as the apple of his eye."

The Hebrew word *tappuach*, translated "apple" in the Bible, was used to mean any fruit, just as the Latin word *pomum* was applied to every kind of fruit prior to the seventeenth century, when botanical classification of plants began.

Malus sylvestris, the small crab apple, is the wild ancestor of our cultivated apple. It is found throughout much of Europe and in northwest Asia. Apples were cultivated from ancient times. Michael Zohary, who has studied biblical flora for half a century, states that apples may have been introduced into Israel and Egypt about 4000 B.C. The apricot and bitter orange were introduced much later.

Egyptian papyri of the period of Ramses II (thirteenth century B.C.) indicate that the fields along the Nile delta were full of pomegranate, apple, olive and fig trees. The papyri record the first use of the apple, *depeh* in Egyptian, as food.

A British botanist, expert in biblical plants, states that at one time it was thought that apples would not grow successfully in the Holy Land, but that is not so. Well-preserved, carbonized apples were found in excavations of the ninth century in Kadesh-Barnea, on the Egyptian-Israeli border. The Romans had more than twenty varieties of apples. In the first century A.D. the Roman historian Pliny mentioned numerous apple varieties, including red and white apples from Syria, in his *Naturalis Historia.*

Solomon's "refresh me with apples" may have inspired the nineteenth-century saying, "An apple a day keeps the doctor away." In biblical times Greeks believed the apple healed all disorders. In the second century, Roman court physician Galen prescribed apple wine as a cure-all for almost every ailment. An Arabic author from the same period wrote, "Its scent cheers my soul, renews my strength and restores my breath." Scientists at Yale University have since discovered that the scent of spiced apples produces a calming effect that lowers blood pressure.

Apples are a hallowed remedy for both diarrhea and constipation. Apples and the bark of the tree are used to prevent tooth decay and to help sick children and people suffering from seasickness, faintness, rheumatism, kidney stones and gallstones. An infusion of apple blossoms is given for sore throats and colds.

In biblical times apples were used with raisins for sauces and stuffing. In rose apple salad, grated tart apples were mixed with honey, lemon juice and rose water, garnished with roses and mint, and served with roast lamb or grilled fish.

Meditation

Fruit-basket upset! Lord, that's a game everyone can play! No fear of being left out from the start! I liked and feared that game, Lord. Years later I taught it to hordes of little ones. Their greatest fear was forgetting whether they were apples or oranges or bananas.

Lord, when you walked from village to village, did you praise the Father for the variety of his creation? Did you marvel at the very mystery of seed and fruit? Did you remember the sacred law of your people never to destroy a fruitful tree? What about those trees in paradise and the Father's will to leave a luscious one alone? Truthfully never did understand that one! That was truly a fruit-basket upset if ever there was one!

Well, Lord, it doesn't matter what name my fruit is—only that, in your name, I'm fruitful.

Ficus carica

Fig

"From the fig tree learn its lesson:
as soon as its branch becomes tender and puts forth its leaves,
you know that summer is near."
—Matthew 24:32

The fig tree is the first tree mentioned in Scripture. Adam and Eve "sewed fig leaves together and made loincloths for themselves" (Genesis 3:7) after they ate the forbidden fruit and their eyes were opened.

One of the most important plants in the Bible, the fig is mentioned more than fifty times, at least twelve times in the New Testament. Figs are a sign of fruitfulness and one of the blessings of the Promised Land. Jeremiah uses them as an emblem of good and evil (chapter 24). The fig tree symbolized peace and prosperity: "During Solomon's lifetime Judah and Israel lived in safety,...all of them under their vines and fig trees" (1 Kings 4:25).

Jesus used the fig as an emblem of goodness, "Are grapes gathered from thorns, or figs from thistles?" (Matthew 7:16), and, in the parable of the barren fig tree, as a symbol of spiritual fruitfulness and a reminder of divine mercy (Luke 13:6–9). Figs and fig trees were so indispensable that any parable connected with them was bound to impress the hearer.

The last mention of figs is in Revelation 6:13: "and the stars of the sky fell to the earth as the fig tree drops its winter fruit when shaken by a gale."

Its high sugar content made the nutritious delicacy one of the most important foods in Bible times. Unlike most other fruits, figs ripen gradually and are picked from May to October. The first fruits appear simultaneously with the leaves in the spring and are especially prized. The late summer crop is dried and made into cakes or kept on strings.

The Torah was compared to a fig tree. The tree is picked gradually and so it is with the Torah, according to Bamidbar Rabba, "one learns a little today and much on the morrow, for one cannot learn it in one or two years." Studying the Torah was like picking figs: "the more you search the tree, the more figs you find, and the more you study Torah, the more you find in it."

Teenah, the Hebrew word for "fig tree," means "to spread out." A prophetic rabbinic homily said that Jerusalem would spread out on all sides from its short trunk, the City of David, just as the fig tree spreads its branches on all sides. There were specific names for the fruit. The plural *teenim* referred to figs as fruit. Green or unripened fruit were *pag* or *pageha*, and the first ripe figs were *bikkurah*, meaning "one who watches." A cake of dried figs was *debelah* or *d've-lim*. Bethany means "house of figs" and Bethpage means "a house of green figs."

Dried figs dating from 5000 B.C. were found at the excavation of Gezer, on the western slopes of the Judean mountains. Figs have been cultivated since the Early Bronze Age, around 3000 B.C. Iron Age remains were found at Beth-shemesh near Jerusalem and appear in the Nineveh relief of the siege of Lachish. First-century A.D. remnants were found at Masada.

In Egypt the first recorded use of figs as food and medicine is during the Second Dynasty (2700 B.C.). An offering table depicted on an Eighteenth Dynasty wall painting from the tomb of Nebamun, in Thebes, shows figs, grapes and cucumbers.

The fig is one of the few biblical plants whose medicinal value is mentioned in the Bible. We read that Isaiah ordered that a lump of figs be applied to King Hezekiah's boil "so that he may recover" (2 Kings 20:7).

Figs were used in Egyptian medicine from the most ancient times, internally as a purgative and for various stomach diseases and externally for stiffness and back pains. The Assyrians used figs in a poultice or plaster, as in Hezekiah's case. Boiled in milk or barley water, it was taken for coughs and chest pains. It is used in folk medicine for cancer, for skin conditions such as warts and corns and for healing wounds.

Meditation

So, Lord, what do you really mean when you want us to be fruitful? In one place you tell us it is to have faith and do something, meaning, move it by prayer. That's right after you withered the fig tree (Matthew 21:18–22). In another place there will be fruitfulness if we stay attached to you (John 15:4–5). Then there is the teaching on dying to self like seeds (John 12:24). Listening well and trying to understand also bears fruit (Matthew 13:23).

Paul tackles the question, too. He tells us to lead a life worthy of you, Lord, as we "bear fruit in every good work and as [we] grow in the knowledge of God" (Colossians 1:10), and he tells the Romans, "If the part of the dough offered as first fruits is holy, then the whole batch is holy; and if the root is holy, then the branches also are holy" (11:16).

Am I getting it right, Lord, you surely do want us to be fruitful, somehow, like it was with Mary? You were her fruit. So, if I am grafted to you and stay there, listening really well to what you say, and doing your will as best I can, then this fruit is going to happen, you will be born in heart after heart, as naturally as good trees bear figs that will last.

Punica granatum

Pomegranate

"Your channel is an orchard of pomegranates
with all choicest fruits."
—Song of Solomon 4:13

With its dark green foliage, crimson flowers and red fruit, the pomegranate tree was grown for its beauty as well as for its fruit, and the Song of Solomon extolled both: "Your cheeks are like halves of a pomegranate" (4:3).

Pomegranates figure prominently as decoration in the Bible. Embroidered pomegranate flowers in the form of bells alternated with the fruit around the lower edges of the blue *ephod*, or "robe" of the high priest (Exodus 28:33). Pomegranates were embroidered on the high priest's mitre or ceremonial turban. Solomon's crown was modeled after the calyx above the fruit. The capitals atop each of the two pillars on the porch of Solomon's Temple were adorned with two hundred carved pomegranates (1 Kings 7:20).

The fruit and flowers were beautiful models for other ornamental carvings. The staves holding the Torah were decorated with *rimonei ha-torah,* pomegranate crowns of the Torah. A visitor to the Holy Land almost one hundred years ago describes "a wonderful pomegranate ornament on the walls of an old Jewish temple in Capernaum in which Jesus is said to have preached." The rich carvings of pomegranates, figs and grapes can still be seen in the stonework remains lying near the temple ruins.

Jewish tradition says that the perfect pomegranate contains 613 seeds, one for each commandment in the Bible. The expression, "full as a pomegranate," refers to someone brimful of good deeds. In folklore every fruit is believed to contain one seed that has come from Paradise.

Rimmon is the Hebrew name for the tree and its fruit. Several towns and villages in Palestine bearing the name of Rimmon and En-rimmon, "spring of the pomegranate," are mentioned in Scripture (Joshua 15:32, 1 Chronicles 4:32, Zechariah 14:10, Nehemiah 11:29).

The cultivation of pomegranates in ancient Palestine and Egypt is well documented. Plant remains of pomegranates, dates, walnuts, lentils, wheat, onion and garlic dating from the Chalcolithic period (between 3820 and 2820 B.C.) were found in the Cave of the Treasure in Nahal Mishmar near the Dead Sea. Pomegranates were found in other sites near the Dead Sea, in the Eighteenth Dynasty tomb of Kha at Deir el-Medina, in caves near En-Gedi and at the ruins of Gezer. An attractive wooden bowl in the form of a pomegranate and recognizable remains of the fruit were found in excavations of Jericho of around 1650 B.C. The first record of the fruit's use as food and medicine in Egypt is in the Twelfth Dynasty (2052–1778 B.C.). Leaves, used in mummy garlands, and pomegranates are found in Eighteenth Dynasty tombs, and wall paintings in the Botanical Chamber of Thutmosis II depict pomegranates. Medical papyri of 1200 B.C. indicate it was used in herbal medicine.

Prime medicinal uses of the pomegranate were for expelling tapeworms, for skin problems and for diarrhea. A mouthwash from an infusion of flowers was used for sore throats and gingivitis. The rind was burned to disinfect and fumigate houses and other buildings. The fruit contains antitumor agents and an estrogen hormone.

Pomegranates ripen at the end of the summer and are traditionally eaten on Rosh Hashanah, the Jewish New Year. They were used in sauces for lamb or chicken, and the seeds were eaten with sugar or made into a spiced wine. The juice, sometimes mixed with wine, made a refreshing drink. Grenadine syrup is made from the seeds.·

The botanical name, *Punica*, is the Latin name for Carthaginians, so it is thought that the pomegranate is native to that area. Pliny said three kinds existed there, white, red and a larger and more astringent kind, used mainly in medicine. One writer says the ancients called it the Carthaginian apple.

Meditation

"Come, my beloved,

 let us go forth into the fields,

 and lodge in the villages;

let us go out early…

 and see whether…

 the pomegranates are in bloom.

There I will give you my love." (Song of Solomon 7:11–12)

Lord, there are times to be with you and not speak nor ask nor let anything disturb this utter presence. It would kill the preciousness of the moment to ask, "What do you mean?" There is a seeing and a sensing beyond words. Best to let the symbols have their secrets. Reading Solomon's song is like that for me: image after image to express the presence of the beloved where words are as limited as a shadow to the real experience.

The pomegranate is like that. A thing of beauty in blossom and form and bittersweet to taste—but I'm not sure my cheeks should really look like that bumpy rind and those pocky seeds! I've got to be silent and taste the symbol. Then there is love.

85   *FRUITS OF THE FIELD*

Incense and Anointing Oils

"The LORD spoke to Moses: Take the finest spices:
of liquid myrrh five hundred shekels,
and of sweet-smelling cinnamon half as much,
that is, two hundred fifty, and two hundred fifty of aromatic cane,
and five hundred of cassia—measured by the sanctuary shekel—
and a hin of olive oil; and you shall make of these
a sacred anointing oil blended as by the perfumer;
it shall be a holy anointing oil."

—*Exodus 30:22–25*

*T*he Israelites were still in the desert, on their way to the Promised Land, when the Lord instructed Moses to make holy anointing oil and incense. The anointing oil was to be used for consecrating the Tent of Meeting, the Ark of the Covenant and the altar as well as the high priest Aaron and his sons, who would be priests. Aaron was to offer the fragrant incense, made as commanded by the Lord in Exodus 30:34–35, on the altar every morning and evening. Personal use of these special compounds was prohibited.

After the temple was built in Jerusalem, incense was offered on the golden altar that stood before the veil of the Holy of Holies and the burning of incense became part of the daily services in the Temple. Luke 1:8–10 tells of the priest entering the sanctuary of the Lord to offer incense while the people prayed outside.

The anointing of priests continued and later kings were also consecrated. Saul, David and Solomon were anointed as part of their coronation ceremonies. Early Christians did not burn incense because of pagan connotations (the Romans ordered Christians to offer incense before the image of the emperor and their gods) and because the strong odor would have led to their detection during times of persecution. Later the use of incense was resumed, and the ritual censing of religious objects and the faithful came to symbolize sanctification.

Secrecy surrounded the blending of the holy oil and incense, compounded according to cryptic formulas of professional perfumers. One of the mystery ingredients of incense was an herb that made the smoke rise in a tall column straight toward heaven. The sacred mixtures were made of costly fragrant substances imported from as far away as Africa, India and China.

Cinnamomum cassia

Cassia

"Vedan and Javan from Uzal entered into trade for your wares:
wrought iron, cassia, and sweet cane were bartered for your merchandise."
—Ezekiel 27:19

The merchants of Tyre bartered for cassia and sweet cane, two of the ingredients in the holy anointing oil. Cassia has not been found in Egyptian tombs, suggesting that it was probably also not present in ancient Israel. Biblical botanists believe it was imported from China or Sri Lanka and probably reached the Mediterranean region in late Old Testament times. Cassia was mentioned by Herodotus in the fourth century B.C. and Dioscorides in the first century A.D. The aromatic substance was burned in the temples of Egypt for fumigation, and recipes for its use were found engraved on the walls of temples.

Cassia was one of the ingredients of the holy anointing oil. The temple shekel was the standard weight of measurement, equivalent to 10 grams or .351 ounces. Five hundred shekels of cassia would weigh 10 kilograms or almost 11 pounds.

From the rabbins comes the tradition that a single bottle of sacred oil, found in the Temple of Jerusalem after Antiochus Epiphanes and his forces were driven out, was used for lighting the sacred lamps of the Temple during the Feast of Rededication in 164 B.C. The oil lasted eight days, the duration of the feast, which was held in honor of the restoration of worship in the Temple.

Cassia is one of the fragrant spices mentioned in Psalms 45:8: "your robes are all fragrant with myrrh and aloes and cassia." It was one of the ingredients in perfumes for personal use. The pleasant aromas were not only pleasing but their germicidal and anti-fungal qualities were important for personal health and hygiene. To perfume originally meant to fumigate.

The Hebrew words *qiddah* (*kiddah*) and *ketziah*, translated as "cassia," may refer to two different plants or spices, but ketziah is generally thought to refer to the cassia bark tree, *Cinnamomum cassia*. Cinnamon and cassia bark trees are similar tropical evergreens, both having glossy, leathery leaves, growing to heights of forty feet and requiring hot, humid conditions. Cassia bark has been substituted for cinnamon but is considered inferior because of its coarser texture and more pungent aroma and taste. It is also known as Chinese cinnamon.

In Assyria cassia was used instead of cinnamon as a digestive aid and for toothaches. Pulverized cassia is mentioned in a treatment for eye disease in a medical clay tablet from about 2000 B.C., and a seventh-century B.C. text recommends a bandage soaked in cassia juice and two unknown drugs for inflamed eyes. Cassia is now used to treat diabetes, pain, fever and rheumatism.

Cassia buds, dried immature fruits, resemble cloves and substitute for cloves for seasoning dishes. Herbalists recommend cassia buds and leaves with ginger or coriander as a purgative. The oil, distilled from the fruit as well as the leaves and twigs, is used for flavoring and in pharmaceutical products. It is considered a precious perfume and mixed with other flowers to make a potpourri. The spice is obtained from the inner bark of the tree, which dries and peels off after incisions are made in the branches.

Meditation

Thinking about oil today, Lord. Got a drop of butter on a Sunday-best dress. Did you know that oil spots never seem to really go away? When the wind blows, that spot shows up every time. Catches dust, draws attention—at least mine! Spilled a drop of cooking oil on my manuscript, too. Amazed that it would seep through twenty pages overnight.

But what about you, Lord, when we call you Christ, the anointed one by God's Spirit, and call ourselves Christians? How deep does that oil go? And is it attractively fragrant? More fragrant than the secrets of the cassia?

Commiphora abyssinica, Cistus incanus
Myrrh

"Then, opening their treasure chests,
they offered him gifts of gold, frankincense, and myrrh."
—Matthew 2:11.

Myrrh is associated with Jesus at his birth and at his death. The Wise Men brought myrrh, foretelling Jesus' suffering and death. While Jesus hung on the cross, a mixture of vinegar and myrrh was offered to him, and after his death Nicodemus brought a "mixture of myrrh and aloes, weighing about a hundred pounds" (John 19:39), to be used in preparing the body for burial.

Highly valued as an aromatic resin, myrrh was an important item of trade. It grew in Gilead in Canaan and in Genesis 37:25 we read of the Ishmaelites coming down from Gilead with myrrh and other spices. They were bound for Egypt, which imported great quantities of frankincense and myrrh from Palestine.

Myrrh was one of the ingredients of the holy anointing oil and also of incense. It served as a fumigant in the temple and was a burial spice.

The Hebrew word *mor,* meaning "bitter," and the Greek word *myrrha* are translated as "myrrh." The myrrh of the Old Testament is generally thought to be ladanum (*lot* in Hebrew), a gum collected from several species of the rockrose (*Cistus creticus, C. incanus*). The Greek traveler and physician Herodotus in the fifth century B.C. says it was gathered from the beards of he-goats, where it was found sticking like gum, having rubbed off from the bushes on which they browsed. Herdsmen combed the fleeces of their flocks for the precious droplets. Myrrh oil was found in pottery used for the production of perfume in the ruins of En-Gedi, near the Dead Sea.

The densely branched, bushy shrub with hairy green leaves and showy pink or red flowers still grows in Gilead.

In 1570 B.C. Queen Hatshepset of Egypt sent five ships to the Land of Punt, believed to be on the shore of East Africa, in search of spices. Paintings on the walls of her temple in Karnak tell of heaps of myrrh resin and two myrrh trees brought back from that fabled land. That may have been the myrrh of the New Testament, and the trees *Commiphora abyssinica,* thorny shrubs or small trees native to southern Arabia and northeast Africa. Solomon probably grew the trees in his garden, and they still grow in rocky areas, especially in the limestone hills of the Middle East and many parts of North Africa.

Oil-like myrrh drips like tears from the dull-gray bark of the trunks and branches of the myrrh tree and after drying forms irregularly shaped grains of light or dark brown. Dried myrrh is hard and brittle, with a bitter taste.

> My beloved is to me a bag of myrrh
> that lies between my breasts. (Song of Solomon 1:13)

Myrrh was valued as a perfume as well as for its medicinal properties. It was used to perfume clothes, fumigate houses and sweeten the breath. Egyptian women carried "pearls" of myrrh on their persons as a perfume, placing the aromatic gum in a small flask that hung from a chain and rested on their breasts.

In the Greek and Roman worlds, myrrh was a panacea for almost every human ailment from eye infections to hemorrhoids. It served as a local anesthetic (offered to Jesus on the cross) and treated wounds, inflammations, ulcers and stomach problems. It was given to both mother and child for post-natal care, perhaps one reason the Wise Men brought it to Jesus.

Since ancient times myrrh has been used as a mouthwash for sores in the mouth and throat. Present-day myrrh, steam-distilled from the resin, stimulates the immune system, soothes skin conditions, eliminates parasites and alleviates infections and inflammations. The fragrance is said to be uplifting and promote spiritual awareness.

Meditation

Precious myrrh was among your birthday gifts, Lord, and myrrh is twice mentioned at your dying. Bitter fragrance to cleanse and heal and cover the smell of blood and death.

My thoughts turn to you, Mary, as you tell the stories of your son. Your personal gifts to the temple were the gifts of the poor. All the more must these other precious gifts have filled you with wonder! Did you take them to Egypt? Did you use the myrrh to heal his little scratches from childhood play? And did you sing Solomon's verses when you opened the precious oil?

> Until the day breathes,
>   and the shadows flee,
> I will hasten to the mountain of myrrh,
>   and the hill of frankincense.
> You are altogether beautiful, my love;
>   there is no flaw in you. (Song of Solomon 4:6–7)

But, Mary, when you stood by the cross those infinite three hours and your senses perceived myrrh, did you recall those early gifts and now begin to understand his destiny to die? Surely you wished to touch his wounds and sooth them with the oil of healing. But, oh, the wounds were so, so many...

Olea europaea
Olive tree

*"They cast out many demons,
and anointed with oil
many who were sick and cured them."*
—Mark 6:13

The second plant mentioned in the Bible after the fig, the olive tree is important in both the Old and New Testaments. In Genesis 8:11 a dove brings an
olive branch to Noah, a sign that the floodwaters were receding and land was
near. This was also a sign that God's wrath was abating, and since then both
the dove and olive leaf have been symbols of peace and friendship.

One of the most valuable trees of the ancient Hebrews, the olive tree provided oil for anointing the sacred objects in the Temple and for the lamps
that burned there. The Hebrews used it for consecrating priests and kings,
for personal anointing and for cooking, as a salad oil, for illumination and
for healing and beautifying the skin. Ceremonial use of olive oil continues as
Jews light candles, representing oil lamps, on the eve of the Sabbath, and in
Christian baptismal and healing ceremonies, ritual blessings and the ordina-
tion of priests.

Olives, olive trees and oil are mentioned at least sixty times in the Bible. This includes references to anointing, since most of the anointing was done with olive oil.

The Hebrew word for "anoint" is *mesiach*, or "messiah" and the Greek word *christos* referred to the practice of "dubbing oil" on athletes following a competition. In 1 Samuel 10:1 we read of the ritual anointing of Saul, the king, and in Psalm 23:5–6 of anointing as a sign of the Lord's goodness and mercy.

In Hebrew *sajit*, the word for "olive tree," means "glossy" or "fresh green" and in the Old Testament the Psalmist exclaims, "But I am like a green olive tree in the house of God" (52:8). In Jeremiah we read, "The Lord once called you, 'A green olive tree, fair with goodly fruit'" (11:16).

Some of the most ancient olive trees grow on Mount Olivet, so named because of the abundance of olive trees growing there. Rising up to the east above Jerusalem, it is mentioned several times in the Bible. It was the place where the Lord stood as he prophesied the future of Jerusalem (Zechariah 14:4). Jesus spent the night there when he was teaching in the Temple (Luke 21:37) and prayed in the Garden of Gethsemane, an olive garden at the foot of Mount Olivet, the night before he died (Matthew 26:36). In Hebrew *gat-shmanim* means "oil press" and *Gethsemane* means "the garden with the olive press." After Christ's resurrection the disciples witnessed his ascension to heaven from Mount Olivet (Acts 1:9–12).

In New Testament times the sick and dying were anointed with oil. Mark tells us that the apostles "anointed with oil many who were sick and cured them" (6:13). The Good Samaritan poured oil and wine on the wounds of the man left half dead by robbers (Luke 10:34). In his letter to Jewish Christians, James asks: "Are any among you sick? They should call for the elders of the church and have them pray over them, anointing them with oil in the name of the Lord" (5:14).

Valuable as gold, the olive tree has been cultivated more than six thousand years and was so well known that at the time of the flood it could be recognized by a single leaf. It flourishes even on bare rocks, requires little water and endures drought, making it a symbol for endurance. The tree continues to send up shoots from the base of the trunk, even when the trunk has been cut down, as happened when Titus cut down all the trees during the siege of Jerusalem in A.D. 70. Branches continue to bear fruit even though the trunk is gnarled, bent and hollow. Some of the trees in the Garden of

Gethsemane are thought to have been there in Jesus' time.

Helen Frenkley, in a guidebook for Neot Kedumin, the 625-acre biblical land reserve in Israel, describes the olive tree and its symbol:

> The lightest breeze crowns the olive trees with a silver halo that moves like a wave of light over the trees as the wind inverts the leaves. The underside of each olive leaf is covered with tiny whitish scales, while its upper side is dark green. When the wind rustles the leaves of the olive tree, this contrast of shades produces a unique silvery sheen. The light of the olive tree itself, together with the clear white flame produced by burning olive oil, made the olive the symbol of "light to the world," a symbol that helps explain the prophet Zechariah's vision of the menorah. [Zechariah saw a menorah of gold, with two olive trees beside it, one on each side.]

Remains of olives dating from the Early Bronze Age, fourth century B.C., were found in the Cave of the Treasure in Nahal Mishmar north of the Dead Sea. They precede findings from ancient Egypt and Crete. In biblical times almost every village had an olive grove and olive press, and ancient presses can still be found in densely bushed areas. A revolving stone crushed the olives, and the oil spurted from under the stone into a cistern dug into the ground. One source says that olives were crushed by hand for the Temple oil.

Ancient surgeons used olive leaves for plasters and liniments to treat wounds and bruises. The oil protected hair and skin from the ravages of wind and sun, and shepherds used it to heal the bruised heads of their animals. Olive oil is used to treat numerous conditions, among them burns, colds, sore throats, dermatitis and rheumatism. It softens the skin and prevents heart disease. Olive leaf tea is recommended for gout and fevers. In ancient folk wisdom "olive oil makes all your aches and pains go away." The Bach flower remedy is given to restore peace to a distressed and tired mind and give strength to an exhausted body.

Meditation

Found out today, Lord, pure olive oil costs a lot. Fine olives, too. Wanted to put them on a party tray and thought twice. Now I know the planners who serve the olive go the extra mile for the finest hour.

All these associations draw me back in time to that Last Supper and its aftermath—the lamb, the bitter herbs, the wine, the bread—and then the walk to the garden to pray and wait. During those early night hours did it comfort you to be in the garden where the olive press was? Did you see the press and know its symbol? Did that original garden come to your mind and heart, and were you ready to restore our ability to walk with the Father in the garden?

Lord, even if I sleep, may I come to the garden with you?

INCENSE AND THE ANOINTING OILS

Lilies of the Field

*"...Consider the lilies of the field, how they grow;
they neither toil nor spin, yet I tell you,
even Solomon in all his glory
was not clothed like one of these."*
—Matthew 6:28–29

The lilies of the field are not only lilies but refer to several different plants that grew wild in the Holy Land in biblical times. In the early spring the fields near the Sea of Galilee are filled with anemones, tulips, poppies, crocuses, narcissis and gladiolis as well as some lilies. These are the lilies of the New Testament. Iris, hyacinth and several varieties of lily, Madonna lily, Martagon lily and water lily, are said to be the lilies of the valley, the lilies of the Old Testament.

Scholars suggest that when Jesus asked his audience to "consider the lilies of the field," he was referring to those well-known flowers growing in the fields near Galilee where he was speaking. Both the red anemone and the scarlet Martagon lily could be the flower more glorious than Solomon's robes.

The early spring flowers are collectively named *nitzanim* in the Song of Solomon 2:12, "The flowers [*nitzanim*] appear on the earth." The word may derive from the verb *hanetz*, which means "to come into blossom." The Hebrew spring month *Nissan* is named for the spring blooming of the nitzanim.

In Palestine folklore there is a special name for wildflowers, *hannun*, the true meaning of which is "a beautiful wild flower." This name is not applied to "insignificant or colourless flowers" or to garden flowers. Grace M. Crowfoot and Louise Baldensperger, authors of a book on the folklore of plants in Palestine, state,

> Of all the lovely flowers they honour with the name, the red anemone is the hannun *par excellence*. This is the flower the fellah would regard as more glorious than Solomon with his "scarlet clad soldiers with gold dust in their hair."

In earliest times hills and slopes were covered with wild thickets and bushes and many varieties of wildflowers grew there. When the Israelites entered the Promised Land, they cleared large sections of the land of Canaan, planting vineyards and groves of olives and fruit trees. After the Jews were exiled and once-fertile fields lay fallow, wildflowers grew up again, covering plains and hillsides.

Flowers were not commonly used in religious rites but they were valued for decoration and for their scent: "My beloved is to me a cluster of henna blossoms" (Song of Solomon 1:14).

Anemone Coronaria, A. pulsatilla

Anemone, Windflower

The flower's generic name comes from the Greek word *anemos*, meaning "the wind." According to Pliny, first-century Roman scholar, anemones flowered only when the wind was blowing. In his day the anemone was called *herba venti* (wind herb) and magicians gathered the flowers as a remedy against disease, placing the flowers around the neck or arm of a sick person to cure illness. The name also comes from the Sanskrit word *anti*, which means "he breathes." In the Near East the flower was a symbol for disease and it was thought that that flower actually carried disease. In early European times the peasants believed that this flower poisoned the air and they would hold their breath while running past a field of anemones.

Legends tell that the anemones in Palestine were white or blue until the crucifixion of Christ, when some blood dropped from the cross on Golgotha and stained the blossoms growing at his feet, that the crimson flower then sprang up from the blood of Christ at the foot of the cross and that it grows on the graves of innocent victims of injustice. In the East the flower was associated with death and grief and was used in burial ceremonies. In 100 B.C. the Greek poet Bion wrote, "And where a tear has dropped, the wind-flower blows."

It is said that the seed was in the soil brought back on ships returning from the Holy Land during the Crusades. Umberto, Bishop of Pisa, had suggested the "sacred earth" be carried instead of the sand usually used as ballast on the ships. Sometime after the earth was spread on the Campo Santo, (the "holy ground," or graveyard) the plant appeared, "as if sprung from the blood of martyrs." This was regarded as a miracle, and pilgrims carried the seed of the precious flower from monastery to monastery, distributing the plant throughout Europe.

The species name, *Coronaria*, comes from the fact that the ancient Greeks and Romans used the flower in crowns, wreaths and garlands. One of the most conspicuous plants of the Holy Land, the anemone can be found blooming on the shores of the Lake of Galilee and on the plains and foothills beyond. It is a tuberous plant with showy blooms of scarlet, purple, rose, yellow and white. The flowers open in the morning and close at night.

The sixteenth-century herbalist John Gerard said, "All the kinds of anemone are sharp, biting the tongue...." It is considered poisonous except when given in extremely small doses, and even touching the plant can cause irritation.

Anemone pulsatilla is called the pasqueflower because it blooms in the spring and sometimes on Easter (*Pasqua*) Sunday. Also called the windflower, this plant has large blue to red-purple bell-shaped flowers with bright yellow anthers.

In homeopathic medicine *Anemone pulsatilla* is the remedy used for persons with rapid mood changes and constantly changing symptoms. The flower essence, used in aromatherapy, promotes feelings of inner strength and stability.

In France it has been used as a sedative and for treating coughs. American Indians used the root or leaf tea as a poultice for wounds and sores and placed the roots under their pillows to induce dreams. According to Arabic folk medicine the flowers were once used for stomach tumors.

Meditation

What I cherish today, I toss and trample tomorrow. My laurels woven with splendid color whither and die. They mean nothing after a while. Words of love and faithfulness, Lord—are they lost in wind's breath? Oh, the ceaseless sway of my heart in the rising-subsiding of the wind.

I need to taste your bitterness, anemone, to grow strong and calm and firm. Will I ever be worthy of the crown the Creator wishes to weave for me? Take my heart's wayward fickleness, weave it with steadfastness, heal its endless ache—at least until tomorrow.

Papaver rhoeas

Poppy

One of the most common flowers in the fields of Israel, the corn poppy produces beautiful red flowers that open each morning and close each evening. Blossoms last only two or three days, their life and beauty fading quickly, like the flowers of the field in Isaiah 40:6, 8 (also 1 Peter 1:24–25), symbolizing the ephemeral nature of things in contrast to the enduring word of God:

> All people are grass,
> > their constancy is like the flower of the field.
> The grass withers, the flower fades;
> > but the word of our God will stand forever.

In the first century, Flavius Josephus, author of *Jewish Antiquities,* wrote that the poppy was one of several plants embroidered on the high priest's mitre, or ceremonial turban. The headdress consisted of a second cap, with blue embroidery and a crown of gold, fastened over the traditional cap worn by priests. Henbane, turnip, rocket, pomegranate and siderites were also embroidered on the mitre.

The annual corn poppy is one of the flowers included in the *nitzanim* (spring flowers) of the Song of Solomon. The plant grows like a weed in the wheat fields of Israel, blooming before harvest time, while the grain is still green.

In Artas, a village near Bethlehem, early in the last century, the old folk called the poppy *el behkhita,* or "lucky one" and *khash khash*, meaning "rattle," because it resembled a child's rattle. The children played a game called Fortune Teller with the buds, asking a question before opening each one.

According to papyri dating from 1443 B.C., the poppy was among the medicinal plants commonly used in Egypt. Taken internally it was used to quiet crying children, and externally it treated head ailments, running wounds and boils. Poppies were among the plants in preserved funeral garlands found on mummies, and poppies as well as anemones from the second century B.C. were found in Eighteenth dynasty tombs and at Deir el- Medina in Egypt.

Gerard, sixteenth-century herbalist, said the "Corne-Rose" or "wilde Poppy" was called *Papaver rhoeas* in Latin "because the floure thereof soon falls away." *Rhoeas* was an old Italian name given to a fabled priestess, the mother of Romulus and Remus (Rhea Silvia) and to Cybele, the Anatolian mother-goddess later associated with the Greek Demeter.

The bright red corn poppy, which likes to grow on disturbed land, such as plowed or battle ground, appeared on battlefields in Europe from the seventeenth century through World War I, becoming a symbol of fallen warriors and soldiers. Legends tell that in Belgium a scarlet stream of healing poppies covered the battlefields in 1694, the year following the battle of Neerwinden, and the fields of Waterloo were thick with the red flowers after Napoleon's defeat by the English in 1815.

The Flanders poppy became a symbol of remembrance and an emblem of both world wars after Dr. John McCrae wrote these lines following the 1915 battle of Ypres in Belgium:

> In Flanders fields the poppies blow
> Between the crosses, row by row,
> That mark our place.

If ye break faith with us who die
We shall not sleep, though poppies grow
In Flanders fields.

In modern medicine the petals, seeds and leaves are used as a gentle sedative and their calming action helps colic, sleeplessness, tension headaches and high blood pressure. A gargle helps coughs and sore throats. The flower essence assists in deepening one's inner, spiritual life. The seeds are used for seasoning bread and cakes.

The yellow-orange flowering California poppy (*Eschscholzia californica*), used medicinally by Native Americans and early settlers much like the corn poppy, is the state flower of California and native to the western part of North America.

Papaver somniferum, the opium poppy, is thought to be the gall added to vinegar and offered to Jesus on the cross.

Meditation

A wonderful thing to behold, Lord! The first time I saw it, the beauty took my breath away. The brilliance of the red poppy is sheer gift tucked among the green ripening wheat. I wanted to stand and look for hours until my companions asked: "Won't the poppy seeds spoil the purity of the wheat?" Laughter broke the spell of being caught up in this lovely sight. Another said: "Think of poppy seed coffee cake!" As we walked away, Lord, I thought: The two match well—wheat ground to finest flour and tiny seeds painstakingly harvested. But, it's true, the mix and match in the field becomes the farmer's dilemma.

How confusing, Lord! Beauty in the field is pain for the farmer, but the two together in the end is something delicious. I wonder, will it be like that in eternity—that acknowledged sin rooted out and healed will spice the eternal banquet delightfully?

Crocus sativus

Crocus

The crocus is one of the first wildflowers to appear in the spring, and as the days grow longer, many parts of Palestine are brilliant with the flowers of more than a dozen kinds of crocuses. Blossoms of white, pink, purple, blue and orange-yellow dot the fields and even the desert. Henry Osborne, a biblical botanist of the mid–nineteenth century, saw orange-yellow crocuses growing wild on Mount Tabor.

> The desert shall rejoice and blossom;
> like the crocus it shall blossom abundantly.... (Isaiah 35:1)

Anemones and crocuses store their food and energy in corms, much like the bulbs of tulips and narcissus, and multiply as new corms form. Pliny's statement, "Saffron loves to be beaten and trodden underfoot, and in fact, the worse it is treated the better it thrives," suggests that the corms produce more offsets if they are deliberately injured.

Roasted corms are a delicacy in Artas, where a proverb warns that once the leaves dry up it will be difficult to find where the plant has been, therefore "In March pull up crocus night and day." Children make wreaths of the plaited leaves, with the corms hanging from them like beads, and sell them in the market.

Crocus, the generic name, comes from the Greek word *krokus,* derived from the Hebrew *karkom.* Rich orange-yellow stigmas of several varieties of crocuses are used to produce the saffron herb and spice. The word *saffron* is an Anglicized form of the Arabic word *zafran,* meaning "yellow."

In biblical times saffron was used as a condiment and perfume. Saffron crocus (*Crocus sativus*) was one of the fragrant, spice-producing plants and trees that grew in King Solomon's garden: "Your channel is an orchard of... [spike]nard and saffron, calamus and cinnamon" (Song of Solomon 4:13–14).

Talmudic references to *karkom* are for a plant, thought to be *Crocus sativus,* whose flowers were used for coloring and healing purposes. Saffron appears in a Thebes papyrus from 1553 B.C. and a list of Assyrian medicinal plants. It was used externally as a fumigant and internally as a tonic and to treat cramps and colic.

The plant, found in Palestine from very early times, is thought to have originated in Asia Minor or Greece and been imported into Palestine during the early Hebrew monarchy. A fresco from about 1500 B.C. found in the House of the Frescoes in Knossos on the island of Crete shows a saffron gatherer at work.

In ancient Greece and Rome saffron was used in medicine and cooking, as a cosmetic dye and for its perfume. Pliny reports that the benches and floors in public theaters were strewn with saffron, and the petals placed in small fountains to disperse the scent in large halls. Saffron was also used to decorate marriage beds.

In the fourth century A.D. Emperor Constantine sent the bishop of Rome a gift of spices that included saffron, cloves and pepper.

Gerard said saffron helps those with consumption and strengthens the heart. In medieval England it was grown commercially at Saffron Walden and Saffron Hill.

Saffron has been used to treat cancer and is thought to lower blood pressure. The Lebanese make a tea of saffron crocus stigmas for children suffering from chicken pox, measles and mumps.

Estimates are that it takes the stigmas of about forty-three hundred flowers to make an ounce of saffron, the world's most expensive spice. The Spanish use it in paella, the French in bouillabaisse and the Milanese in risotto. Saffron is used in Indian curries.

The blue-flowered saffron crocus is one of about twenty species that blooms in the fall.

Meditation

I stand amazed about your crocuses, Lord! Little spring-time garden flower, tiny victory in a northern March, who would have thought you are of greater value than gold? Your three stigmas are gathered by hand. Thousands of you are needed for one ounce of your essence, an essence that serves purpose after purpose.

Lord, will I one day stand amazed at all the things I do not know and do not properly value—things of your goodness, of your beauty, of your love? Awaken me each day to love these gifts and the gentle hands that reap their harvest!

Lilies of the Valley

"I am a rose of Sharon,
a lily of the valleys."
—Song of Solomon 2:1

Brightly colored flowers covered the hills and valleys in biblical times. Forests vanished as centuries of exploitation and neglect of the land took their toll, but flowers from bulbs, tubers and corms survived the dry summers. Now remote places on rocky limestone hillsides provide ecological niches for a variety of perennial plants, some thought to be long extinct or not indigenous to the land. The Madonna lily, the hyacinth and eight species of iris are most prevalent among the modern-day flora of the Mediterranean part of Palestine.

The Hebrew phrase *shoshanat ha'amakim* is commonly translated as "lilies of the valley." A nature photographer in Israel believes that the white lily is a probable candidate for the expression "lily of the valley," which indicates an extremely beautiful bloom. Iris, hyacinth and several varieties of lily, Madonna lily, Martagon lily and water lily, are said to be the lilies of the valley, the lilies of the Old Testament. The "rose of Sharon" is actually a tulip that grows in the Sharon Valley.

These flowers probably grew in the garden of King Solomon, who reigned from 962 to 922 B.C., and were among those mentioned in the Song of Solomon, attributed to Solomon but actually written several hundred years later.

The love poetry of the Song of Solomon is in the form of dialogue between a young shepherd and his beloved shepherdess, both probably from the northern parts of Israel. Images of nature and its fruit, flowers, spices and trees embody the beauty and charms of the beloved. The Song of Solomon came to be regarded as a love song between Israel and the Creator, expressing God's love for his people, leading Rabbi Akiva to state: "If all the books of the Bible are holy, the Song of Songs is the holy of holies" (Mishna, Yadayim).

Later the Song of Solomon symbolized Christ's relationship to his people, the church and the individual soul. Passages were applied to the Blessed Virgin Mary in liturgy and prayer, especially the Little Office, or Office of the Blessed Virgin Mary. Medieval painters often depicted Mary in an enclosed garden: "A garden locked is my sister, my bride" (4:12).

Hyacinthus orientalis

Hyacinth

"...he pastures his flock among the lilies."
—Song of Solomon 2:16

In Godspeed's translation of the Song of Solomon, we read of "a hyacinth of the valleys" and young deer that pasture among the hyacinths.

Some scholars believe that at least some of the Bible's "lilies" are really wild hyacinths, which grow in rocky places in the Holy Land. The thick, scrubby underbrush of the maquis in the eastern part of Palestine, from the Lebanon to the Judean mountains, provides shelter to many bulb and tuber plants, among them the hyacinth. In the springtime the exquisite blooms of the wild hyacinth, always deep blue and very fragrant, cover the hillsides around Lake Galilee.

The generic name comes from a Greek god of spring vegetation, Hykinthos, loved by both Apollo and Zephyrus. Various versions of the story relate that Hykinthos was killed by Apollo out of jealousy, unintentionally killed by Apollo or died after accidentally hitting himself with the discus during a game. Apollo then created the flower from the blood of his friend.

Grieving, Apollo sighed the universal Eastern mourning wail, "Ai, ai," and the letters adorned the sepals of the flower. Because *ai* was similar to the Greek word for "eternal," the hyacinth was often carved on Greek tombs and signified remembrance.

Hyacinths were first found growing in Asia Minor, as suggested by the species name *orientalis*. They were cultivated in Turkey and Persia.

In Christian symbolism the flower represents a desire for heaven, peace of mind and prudence. Hyacinths were dedicated to the Virgin Mary.

The Greeks used hyacinth to treat dysentery and the bite of poisonous spiders. Gerard, herbalist of the 1500s, writes that the roots, "after the opinion of Dioscorides, being beaten and applied with white wine, hinder or keep backe the growth of haires." The seeds are used to treat jaundice, and tea made from the bulbs is given medicinally in Lebanon.

Meditation

Mary, they say hyacinths call you to mind. I wonder why. Blue, perhaps, fragrant from afar, springtime awaiting the one who is to come. I wonder if the lily shape of the clustered blossoms has anything to do with it? Which brings me to the point—clustered blossoms tightly joined, yet fully free to open and develop one little lily after another, none crowding out the other. But what a compact unity! Communion of identity.

Surely, Mary, hyacinths don't love, but like you, they can show what giving of self can accomplish—one blossom nested near the other in peace and in the beauty of letting each one be. The fragrance of such unity is far-reaching and splendid.

Lilium candidum

Madonna Lily

"My beloved has gone down to his garden,
to the beds of spices,
to pasture his flock in the gardens,
and to gather lilies."

—*Song of Solomon 6:2*

Only a flower of such outstanding beauty as the stately white lily would grow in the specialized gardens of the wealthy and powerful Solomon. Found eight times in the Song of Solomon, the lily is associated with images of love, beauty and nourishment. First Kings 7:19 describes the ornamental use of the blossom's likeness in Solomon's Temple: "Now the capitals that were on the tops of the pillars in the vestibule were of lily-work, four cubits high." The brim of the "molten sea," or great cistern, was "made like the brim of a cup, like the flower of a lily; it held two thousand baths" (7:26).

The Hebrew word *shushan*, usually translated as "lily," means a beautiful flower. The word may derive from *shesh*, the root word for "six," which matches the number of petals of the white Madonna lily.

Considered to be the true biblical lily by a majority of ancient and medieval writers, the Madonna lily is the most often mentioned flower in Scripture. But the Swedish naturalist Hasselquist and other eighteenth- and nineteenth-century botanists and travelers found no true lily in Palestine. Scholars thought the plant had been incorrectly identified until 1925, when M. N. Naftolsky, a well-known Israeli plant hunter, found it growing on the walls of a moist limesink in the mountains of upper Galilee.

The Madonna lily, which needs moisture and shade to flourish, was plentiful in Palestine in biblical times but gradually disappeared following the decimation of forests and the drying up of creeks and streams. The plant has been found in the wild on Mount Tabor. It still grows in Galilee and on Mount Carmel, where a botanist described his find in 1945: "Three brilliantly white blooms of this majestic forest plant, on a 121 cm. long stem, shone forth among limestone rocks and the shrubs of moderately dense maqui."

Lilies have been cultivated for over five thousand years, since the Sumerian culture developed in the Tigris-Euphrates valley. One Sumerian city was named Susa, another name for lily.

White lilies adorned the capitals of columns in many ancient civilizations, in Egypt, Assyria and Minoan Crete, as well as in Solomon's Temple in Jerusalem. Greeks called it the "flower of flowers."

In the early days of Christianity, the church dedicated the Madonna lily to the Virgin Mary. She is often depicted holding a lily in her hand in old church paintings. The archangel Gabriel carries the flower in medieval paintings of the Annunciation. Lilies bloom on July 2, formerly the feast of the Visitation, and are thus associated also with that event.

In the apocryphal story, when the priests of the Temple wanted to find a suitable husband for Mary, a Temple virgin, the staves of all the eligible young men were placed in the sanctuary. Lilies blossomed on Joseph's staff. Joseph is sometimes portrayed holding a lily, a symbol of his own virginity.

Legends tell that at first the lilies were yellow, but as the Virgin Mary was walking to the Temple, she stopped to pick some of the flowers, and they turned white at her touch. Walking beside her, Saint Joseph suddenly found his staff sprouting white lilies. Jesus, when he was two years old and called before Moses the pharaoh, held a stem of lilies in his hand. In answer to the pharaoh's questions, the infant waved the lilies toward the river, which flowed with sweet milk. White lilies are a symbol of purity, resurrection, motherhood and peace.

One of the earliest English references to the flower is in the works of Venerable Bede, Benedictine monk and scholar who died in 735. He wrote this poetic description of the Madonna lily as the emblem of the Virgin Mary: "the white petals signifying her bodily purity, the golden anthers the glowing light of her soul."

In ancient Egypt lily-scented ointment was much esteemed, especially if the smell of lilies was strong, as a warming and mollifying agent. The Romans used a concoction made from the bulbs to treat corns and sores on their feet. Mixed with other plants, the roots were used for burns, for snakebite, to clear the complexion and make facial wrinkles disappear and to turn the hair blond. In Lebanon, where the plant grows abundantly, the cooked roots are used for everything from corns to epilepsy. The roots have been used to treat cancer, dermatitis and dropsy. Boiling the bulbs in water produces a facial lotion. The essence of lily promotes inner peace in aromatherapy.

Lilies are edible. To make lily-drop soup, add fresh lily buds to clear chicken soup during the last few minutes of cooking.

Meditation

Some think of purity when they see Madonna lilies. Others think of death, for it is the funeral flower of some nations. Still others think of Easter. Purity! What is this purity that describes you, Mary? There is a church in Rome that has a mosaic on the apse of a side chapel where you stand in a field of lilies. Does purity represent what is clean or what is single-minded, having to do with one great love? Or both? And where do we get the notions of "clean" and "dirty" regarding love intimately expressed?

Perhaps, Mary, another way to think about the lily and you and Joseph is to see the strength of the flower, petals open like a receptive vessel to grace—love from above—a love so overshadowing and powerful that your whole being was simply integral love. And that was enough!

Iris pseudacorus
Yellow Flag Iris

"How glorious he was,...like lilies by a spring of water...."
—Sirach 50:5, 8

Iris, which means "eye of heaven," was the sacred flower of Iris, Greek goddess of the rainbow, and it was told that Iris would take messages from heaven to earth, using the rainbow as a bridge. To ancient Greeks the flower represented faith, valor and wisdom. They placed the iris on the forehead of the Sphinx and fashioned the tip of the royal scepter in the image of an iris.

When King Thutmose III returned home to Egypt in 1479 B.C. after conquering Syria, he held aloft an iris to symbolize his victory. Pictures of irises and other flowers from the king's conquered lands were carved on the walls of his temple, and the iris became a treasured flower in Egypt. Iris flowers have been found in tomb paintings in the Valley of the Kings.

The yellow flag iris, *Iris pseudacorus,* is thought to be the "lilies" mentioned in Hosea 14:5 and the lilies in Sirach 39:14, where faithful children "put forth blossoms like a lily," as well as those in Sirach 50:8. The imagery may reflect the high esteem given the iris by the Greeks and Egyptians, which would have been known to the Hebrews.

Known in France as the fleur-de-lis, the iris led to King Clovis's conversion to Christianity in the fifth century. Besieged by the Germanic Alemanni at the edge of the Rhine, Clovis prayed to his wife's Christian God and then saw that iris grew in the shallow waters of the river. He knew his men could cross there and escape capture.

Early Flemish painters knew the iris as the "sword lily," because of its swordlike leaves, and used it as a symbol for the sufferings of the Virgin Mary during the Passion of her son Jesus. The iris is sometimes substituted for the lily in paintings of the Blessed Virgin, and in Spanish art is used in allusion to her Immaculate Conception.

Romans, Egyptians and Moors grew iris for its medicinal value, using it to treat such varied ailments as epilepsy, chill and fever, headaches, loose teeth and the bite of an adder. Herbalists recommend it for bruises, coughs, violent anger and temper tantrums. Teething infants chew the root, and both infants and their elders wear it as a necklace.

Ancient Greeks used the fragrant roots in manufacturing perfume. Iris roots were lifted from the soil and dried in the shade then placed in linen chests to add perfume and repel moths. Women threaded small pieces of the root on long linen yarns to be hung among their garments. The aromatic roots add a mild scent to tooth powder and hair preparations. The flowers yield a yellow dye, and the roots a black one.

Iris thrives in damp soil and in river and pond margins, often coalescing in extensive masses. It stars the water surface in the shallows of the Hula Nature Reserve, the former Hulch swamp of the northern Jordan Valley. Eight species of iris, along with the Madonna lily and hyacinth, are among the most prevalent plants found in the eastern part of Israel.

Meditation

Then Simeon blessed them and said to his mother Mary, "This child is destined for the falling and the rising of many in Israel and to be a sign that will be opposed so that the inner thoughts of many will be revealed—and a sword will pierce your own soul too." (Luke 2:34-35)

Strong words, painful words, dark words about the child destined for the rise and fall of many, about a sign spoken against, about a sword within you! The iris reminds me of that sword. Mary, what did you feel when you heard Simeon speak like this? Fear, anger, resignation, denial? We really don't know!

What would I have felt? Probably all of the above. One thing is certain, I would have pressed my child tightly to my heart, remembered another message previously, and felt fiercely protective. I would have held to love and promise first. Then wondered about the rest at the turn of every season.

Nymphaea lotus, N. alba

Water Lily, Lotus

*"As the lily among brambles,
so is my love among maidens."*
—*Song of Solomon 2:2*

The lotus of ancient Egypt, sacred to the goddess Isis, once grew abundantly in the lakes of the Nile delta and in pools beside the Upper Nile. It can still be found in the canals of the country. The lotus represented Upper Egypt, while the papyrus denoted Lower Egypt.

With daylight the flowers emerge and rise above the water, expanding toward the sun; in the evening they close their petals and sink beneath the surface, daily reminders of death and rebirth.

In ancient Egypt the lotus symbolized rebirth and immortality, and Egyptian mummies often held lotuses in their hands as a symbol of new life. As far back as 2000 B.C., priests and kings were buried with fresh lotus flowers. A wreath of lotus petals had been placed around the neck of Ramses II. Several layers of the Nile's blossoms often covered the bodies of the deceased.

The lotus was frequently depicted in art, inspiring the Ionic capitals, Greek frets and double frets found in architecture. Numerous representations have been found in tombs. Lotus is one of the foods shown on an offering table in a wall painting from the tomb of Nebamun, Thebes, from the Eighteenth Dynasty. An alabaster lamp stand found in Tutankhamen's tomb is in the form of water lilies.

This beautiful white flower, its large petals streaked with pink, was also known to the Greeks and the Hebrews. The Greeks told of a beautiful nymph, deserted by Hercules, who flung herself into the Nile and was transformed into a white lotus. Homer's *Odyssey* describes a mythical nation where people subsisted totally on lotus and lived in the dreamy indolence induced by their diet.

Found growing wild in the waters of Palestine, the water lily was probably cultivated in Solomon's garden. One writer suggests that the lily of Israel may have been the water lily. Many of the events in the book of Esther occur in the palace in Susa (*shushan* means "lily"), which may have been called the "lily palace."

Petals of the water lily are clearly depicted in ivory plaques found in a royal Israelite palace from the time of Ahab (ninth century B.C.). The blossoms were used as background and in a chain of flowers and buds.

Some biblical botanists suggest that the water lily was the model for the lilies on the columns in Solomon's Temple while others question the use of Egyptian imagery, especially since all of the other plant images used in the Temple (almond, gourd, palm, pomegranate) are plants of the land of Israel.

John Hutton Balfour, who wrote about plants of the Bible in the 1860s, reflects that as water lilies grow vigorously in the waters under the shining southern sun, so Israel, fed by the refreshing streams of living waters, shall flourish under the Sun of Righteousness: "[Israel] shall blossom like the lily" (Hosea 14:5). He compares the "lily among brambles" in Song of Solomon to the church: "Christ refers to his Church as a glorious and sweet flower beside the waters in the midst of a thorny wilderness."

Lotus was one of the herbal remedies used in the pharaonic period. The flower was used in a poultice or unguent with other herbs and spices to treat head injuries, perhaps due to the pleasant aroma. The rhizome was used internally for liver ailments and constipation and as an antidote for poison. The leaves were used externally to treat hair loss and skin diseases. In the Ebers medical papyrus from about 1534 B.C., lotus is listed as a remedy for an obstruction in the belly and for treating the liver.

As a folk remedy, lotus is used for cancer, diarrhea, spasms and tumors. The root mixed with lemon juice was said to remove freckles and pimples and soothe sunburn. The leaves treat hair loss and skin diseases, and leaf tea helps fevers, irritability and diarrhea. American Indians used root tea for coughs, inflamed glands and mouth sores. Egyptian herbalists extol its refreshing and calming effect. In aromatherapy the water lily promotes peace and happiness.

Seeds, roots and stalks of the water lily are still used for food in Egypt. The seeds are ground into bread flour or roasted and eaten like nuts, the rhizomes eaten raw or boiled.

The white *Nymphaea alba* and the blue *N. caerulea,* now quite rare in Israel, can occasionally be seen on the open waters of the Hula Reserve near Lebanon.

Meditation

Lord, did you watch the water lilies at sunrise when you praised your Father before the morning was gone and the work of the day demanded your attention? I once sat at the edge of a pond and the unfolding was like a dance of sheer beauty. Trouble was, Lord, I couldn't leave well enough alone. I wanted to take at least one bit of that beauty with me.

Are you laughing, Lord? You know well what happened! The elusive beauty pulled away in the water. Those lilies are not so easy to pluck! Well, Lord, besides the humiliation of my sopping clothes, my captured splendor simply closed and would not open at home anymore, in spite of my love and admiration for it.

Yes, Lord, your Father freely gives his gifts, if we would but learn to admire them and not to destroy them by our possession.

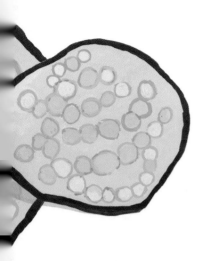

Manna—Bread from Heaven

"He humbled you by letting you hunger,
then by feeding you with manna,
with which neither you nor your ancestors were acquainted,
in order to make you understand
that one does not live by bread alone,
but by every word that comes from the mouth of the LORD."

—Deuteronomy 8:3

The Old Testament tells us that God did not let his people starve, but actually sustained them for forty years in the desert, and with a food that tasted like "wafers made with honey" (Exodus 16:31). Even though the pilgrims eventually complained about the manna, having tired of it, "there is nothing at all but this manna to look at" (Numbers 11:6), it must have been nourishing, and one commentator suggests that "it appears that the cattle survived and prospered."

Scholars who have studied the nineteen references to manna in the Bible have determined that there are three types of manna—some grew up during the night, some fell on the ground at night and yet another kind was purchased or obtained by trade. The word *manna* means "What is this?" None of these types of manna, however, nor the deposits of insects which some consider to be manna, can account for the miracle of the abundant nutriment which sustained thousands of Israelites in the desert for four decades.

In preparation for the Sabbath meal, two braided hallah loaves, wrapped with clean linen cloths, are set on the table. *Hallah* is the name given to the portion of dough that was set aside as an offering for the priests of the ancient Temple of Jerusalem. The two loaves represent the double portion of the manna that the Israelites gathered in the wilderness on Friday to last them through the Sabbath.

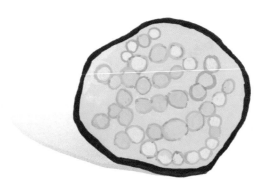

Nostoc
Algae

"When the layer of dew lifted, there on the surface of the wilderness
was a fine flaky substance, as fine as frost on the ground.
When the Israelites saw it, they said to one another, 'What is it?'
For they did not know what it was. Moses said to them,
'It is the bread that the LORD has given you to eat.'"
—Exodus 16:14-15

This form of manna, which grew up during the night when the ground was moist, then withered away and stank in the heat of sun, was produced by a type of tiny blue-green algae called *Nostoc*. In Exodus we are told that the children of Israel gathered up enough for that day; what was left until the next morning bred worms and stank. And each morning more manna was available for them. On the day before the Sabbath they gathered up enough to last through the Sabbath, and that did not stink.

In the Old Testament lore about the "bread from heaven" it is said that the Israelites in the desert were hungry and began to grumble. "You are a stiff-necked people of little faith," Moses said to them. "The Lord will not let you starve." And he told them that from the next day on until they entered the land they were to inherit, they would be fed on manna. When they asked what this manna was, Moses told them it was bread from heaven. "You shall be fed on the food of the angels."

The next morning they found the ground covered sixty cubits high with a grain that looked like hoarfrost, was white as sugar and tasted sweet as honey. They soon learned that it had all the tastes and flavors in the world. It tasted like meat to those who liked meat, like cheese to those who liked cheese. Whatever each person liked best, that was what manna tasted like to them. They also found that no matter how much manna they gathered, when they returned home there was always exactly one omer, or one-tenth of a bushel, for each family member. And the omer contained more food for those who ate much, and less food for those who ate little. The food lasted twenty-four hours, after which it tasted bitter. The manna that remained melted and flowed into the streams. The fish and cattle and birds that drank the waters then tasted a little like manna, so that other nations in the desert had some idea of what manna tasted like.

This tale ends with the information that if the people had been worthy, they would still be living on manna. Also that a measure of manna, along with the rod of Moses, has been preserved in a cave under the holy Temple.

Meditation

Manna, mysterious providing of a mighty God who has a plan.

Manna, the gift of sustenance for a nation uprooted, for strangers wandering toward a promise.

There has to be a rationale—so they say—manna didn't just happen. Lord, they tell us not to mind the simple who believe indeed that it did! But are not these simple ones rich in spirit? How I yearn to be so simple! They are the ones who call what is ordinary "heaven's gift."

There is an awesome truth for the believer who sees the sustainer behind all nourishment. The ordinary is indeed extraordinary.

Lecanora affinis,
L. esculenta,
L. fruticulosa
Lichen

"...he rained down on them manna to eat,
and gave them the grain of heaven.
Mortals ate the bread of angels..."
—Psalm 78:24-25

This manna that fell from the heavens is thought to have been a form of lichen, either *Lecanora affinis, L. esculenta* or *L. fruticulosa*. Botanists say this type of lichen dries up and curls up during periods of drought, then breaks loose from the ground and is transported by the wind. It often falls to earth far from where it originated. In Numbers 11:8 we read that "The people went around and gathered it, ground it in mills or beat it in mortars, then boiled it in pots and made cakes of it; and the taste of it was like the taste of cakes baked with oil."

It is reported that in about 1854, during a famine in Persia, lichen fell from the heavens, providing sustenance for the starving inhabitants. A similar lichen grows on the Sahara Desert and Bedouins collect it for use in sweetening cakes and making bread. Their sheep eat it as well.

Meditation

One of the most fascinating and troublesome aspects of this walk with you, Lord, is the concept of divine providence versus free will. You taught us to ask the Father for our daily bread. You taught us that the Father knows our needs and provides. We are to learn our lesson from the grains of the field. Behind all persons, places, events, simply everything, there is your Father's providing, sustaining hand. And you teach us to seek first the kingdom of God and his righteousness; and all these things shall be given to us.

But, kind Lord, excuse me when I ask the obvious. Why do some have more? And, what about personal responsibility? Am I shirking it or stretching it when I say divine providence is the determining cause for weal or woe? Instruct me well, Lord, that I may see the Father's strong, mighty, loving providence and know how to responsibly, freely interplay with it.

Fraxinus ornus,
Tamarix mannifera
Manna Sap

"They said: here we send you money;
so buy with the money burnt offerings and sin offerings and incense,
and prepare a grain offering...."
—Baruch 1:10

Earlier translations rendered the last phrase of the above Scripture: "prepare ye manna." The Hebrew term for this type of manna was *man*. This manna is thought to have been the gummy exudations of several desert trees, probably the *Fraxinus ornus* (flower ash or manna ash), *Tamarix mannifera* (manna tamarisk), and *Alhagi maurorum* (prickly Alhagi or Sinai manna). One authority suggests it was the *Alhagi camelorum*, or camelthorn.

Several species of ash exude a nutritious and sweet-tasting sap, called *manna*, which has a gentle laxative action and is used for children. In southern Europe the manna ash (*Fraxinus ornus*) is prized for its high yield of manna sap. The bark of the tree is incised with a hook or sickle so that the manna is exuded. Manna from *Fraxinus ornus* is found as flakes (flake manna), fragments (common manna) or as a sticky, viscous mass (fat manna). Manna was once produced commercially in Sicily, with annual production around 750 tons.

Dioscorides said that the "fruit" of the tamarisk (*Tamarix mannifera*) was used as an infusion for the eyes. According the *The Assyrian Herbal*, tamarisk is used to treat the eyes as well as hemorrhages and dysentery.

The sugary secretion that oozed from the leaves and stems of the camelthorn (*Alhagi camelorum*) hardens on contact with the air and is collected over drop cloths. The small, round grains consist of sugar mostly, and are used as a laxative and in folk medicine as a remedy for the chest, polyps and tumors of the abdomen and glands.

Meditation

I placed my hand on the tree and drew it away, sticky, and was annoyed. It will be quite a chore to remove all this sap. How can I be annoyed by your gifts—over and over again! It is my fault. After all, I got in the way of the sap. Lord, I'm intrigued by this stubborn sweet-tasting and fragrant sap! This, too, is meant in the divine plan to be a gift for healing. How I wish my annoyances could be healed and removed, even as I remove this sap.

And what was it your apostle wrote? "Put away from you all bitterness and wrath and anger and wrangling and slander, together with all malice, and be kind to one another, tenderhearted, forgiving one another, as God in Christ has forgiven you. Therefore be imitators of God, as beloved children, and live in love, as Christ loved us and gave himself up for us, a fragrant offering and sacrifice to God" (Ephesians 4:31-32; 5:1-2). Lord, make of the daily annoyances, make of me, a fragrant offering.

Ointments and Perfumes

"I have perfumed my bed with myrrh, aloes, and cinnamon."
—Proverbs 7:17

The Old Testament is full of references to fragrant ointments and perfumes, used for personal hygiene and pleasure, ceremonial anointing and preparing the dead for burial.

Perfumes and ointments were associated with cleanliness and purity in biblical times and were a necessity because of the lack of sanitation and the need to prevent infection. The word perfume comes from the Latin *fumare*, meaning "to smoke"; to *perfume* once meant to "fumigate." Perfumes and incense were used as a disinfectant and to mask the odors of daily life. Jerusalem had a Sheep Gate, a Fish Gate, a Dung Gate and a Horse Gate (Nehemiah 3:1, 3, 13, 28), places where perfumes were especially welcome.

"Perfume and incense make the heart glad...." (Proverbs 27:9)

People perfumed their bodies after bathing and scented their clothes with perfume and spices. They used ointments and pastes made from fragrant woods, herbs and aromatic resins on exposed parts of the body to protect the skin from the sun and wind and climate extremes. They sprinkled their beds and couches with sweet-smelling ointments and spices.

Both the Old and New Testaments refer to the practice of anointing a person as a gesture of respect or honor and for ceremonial occasions. In Mark 14:3 the woman with the alabaster jar containing a costly ointment breaks open the jar and pours the ointment on Jesus' head. John 12:3 tells that "Mary took a pound of costly perfume made of pure nard [and] anointed Jesus' feet."

> Nicodemus, who had at first come to Jesus by night, also came, bringing a mixture of myrrh and aloes, weighing about a hundred pounds. They took the body of Jesus and wrapped it with the spices in linen cloths, according to the burial custom of the Jews.
> (John 19:39-40)

The custom of using aromatic spices and oils to prepare the dead for burial, borrowed from the Egyptians, was necessary because of the hot desert climate. Olive and cedar oils and frankincense, an aromatic resinous gum, were used for embalming. Myrrh and aloes were sprinkled between linen strips and used to wrap the body before burial.

Aquilaria agallocho,
Aloe succotrina
Aloe

"[Y]our robes are all fragrant with myrrh and aloes and cassia."
—*Psalms 45:8*

Scholars distinguish between Old Testament aloes (*Aquilaria agallocho*) and those of the New Testament (*Aloe succotrina*).

The aloes tree, or Lign-aloes-tree, *Aquilaria agallocho*, was a tall and lofty tree, growing up to 120 feet tall with a trunk up to 12 feet in diameter. Known also as the eaglewood tree, it produced a sweet-smelling substance said to be the *ahaloth* and *ahalim* referred to in the Old Testament. The aloes tree, when decayed or diseased, exuded a fragrant oil and resin that was collected for burning as incense, for deodorizing and for use as perfume.

Some scholars believe that the scented white sandalwood tree (*Santalum album*) is the aloe of the Old Testament. Neither eaglewood nor sandalwood was native to the Holy Land, the eaglewood growing in Asia, India and Ceylon, and the sandalwood in India. It is said that aloe juice was imported from

Yemen before aloes were grown in Israel. Yet the aloe in Numbers 24:6, "like aloes that the LORD has planted," was probably a tree native to Palestine, such as the palm, terebinth or oak tree.

The use of aloe can be traced to Egypt. Prospero Alpini, who wrote about ancient Egyptian plants and medicines in the sixteenth century, relates that Egyptian women of his day perfumed their bodies with it. Aloe was known to the Greeks, and it is told that Alexander the Great was persuaded by Aristotle to conquer the island of Socotra for the sole purpose of obtaining sufficient amounts of aloe to heal the wounds of his soldiers.

One nineteenth-century historian of Palestine suggests that Solomon's ships brought it from "the island of its origin," east of the strait of Babel-mandel, and about three hundred miles from the southern coast of Arabia.

> Seamen passing the island can see at a distance the spontaneous growth of the aloe, covering miles of the western shores, with the beauty of their scarlet and yellow flowers tipped with green and in brilliant contrast to the deep green and glossy surface of the leaves.

Aloe succotrina is thought to be the aloe referred to in the New Testament. The succulent plant grew up to five feet in height, and its thick, fleshy gray-green leaves, sometimes two to three feet long, were thick with juice, which when evaporated and solidified was used in healing and embalming. Even the fragrance of freshly gathered leaves, "peculiarly pleasant...unlike that of any other Oriental spice or plant," was considered healthful (Osborn, *Plants of the Holy Land*).

When used by the Jews in wrapping the body for burial, aloe served not only to preserve the body but also to make it fragrant and to express affection for the deceased. The amount brought by Nicodemus, much greater than was customary to use, is thought to have expressed his great reverence for Jesus.

Writers variously state that the plant produced an aromatic juice used in embalming and that one variety of aloes produced a juice with such a bitter smell Nicodemus had to use one hundred pounds of myrrh to neutralize it. Dioscorides mentioned the bitter taste of aloes before describing at great length the medicinal value of the juice. Other writers believe that *Aloe vera* or *Aloe perryi* is the aloe of the New Testament.

The name aloe comes from the Arabic *alloeh* and means "bitter and shiny substance."

Found in the wall carvings of ancient Egyptian temples, aloe is called the plant of immortality.

Mesopotamian clay tablets from 1750 B.C. reveal the use of *Aloe vera* for medicinal purposes. Egyptian records of 550 B.C. mention aloe for skin infections. Dioscorides wrote that aloe juice was beneficial for everything from the "conglutinating of wounds" and "loosening of the belly" to "procuring sleep" and preventing "the hair falling off." The Chinese and ancient Greeks used aloe for constipation.

Aloe is valued for soothing and beautifying the skin. The juice is used in incense, perfume, lotions and scented powder. Some keep plants in their kitchens for the treatment of burns, cutting a portion of leaf and applying the juice directly to the burn. The peeled gel can be applied to inflamed areas of the skin as a first-aid measure in cases of sunburn, frostbite and minor skin irritations. The juice has a strong laxative effect when taken internally. Other medicinal uses include treatment of digestive disorders, asthma and immune system deficiency. Aloe is reported to have anticancer properties.

Meditation

The Master's body, gouged deep with iron-tipped leather lashes, lies dead at the foot of the cross—his side gaping wide where blood and water drain; his feet, his wrists pierced with iron spikes. Agony had climaxed and come to final rest in Mary's arms. Look with Nicodemus's heart upon this scene.

Love and sorrow and loss and shared agony must do something—must clothe the Beloved's nakedness with soothing, healing aloes—even when the Loved One no longer has need of it.

Lord, when you rose from the grave in three days' time, had the aloes and myrrh helped a little to let you know that there were some who had loved you at the hour of your death? How I wish to share the anointing of such love!

Cinnamomum zeylanicum

Cinnamon

"Your channel is an orchard of pomegranates
with all choicest fruits...
calamus and cinnamon...
with all chief spices...."
—*Song of Solomon 4:13-14*

The oldest spice mentioned in the Bible, cinnamon was known in China in 2700 B.C. The cinnamon tree went from China to Persia, then to India, where it became indigenous and was exported to Arabia.

Arabs brought cinnamon and other spices to Egypt along the old caravan routes, pretending it came from the mountains along their southern coast, and told many stories about the difficulty of harvesting to account for its scarcity and high price.

Queen Hatshepset's ships are said to have returned to Egypt from the Land of Punt, on the shores of East Africa, with cinnamon trees in 1570 B.C. About one hundred years later, in Exodus 30:22 Moses is told to use cinnamon and other spices and oils to prepare the holy anointing oil for the Tabernacle. He would have learned about cinnamon's agreeable properties from the Egyptians, who were using it by 1500 B.C.

Cinnamon as an aromatic spice is mentioned in the Old Testament's Song of Solomon and Proverbs. It appears again in Revelation, the last book of the New Testament, in the account of the destruction of Babylon: "And the merchants of the earth weep and mourn for her, since no one buys their cargo anymore, cargo of...cinnamon, spice, incense" (Revelation 18:11–13).

The Hebrew word *kinnamon* is *Kaju manis,* meaning "sweet root," in Malay. The spice comes from the inner bark of the cinnamon tree. Three-year-old branches, which produce the best cinnamon, are incised so that the bark dries and falls off. The bark dries in the shape of cylinders or quills, called *qirfa* by Prospero Alpini, which are tied into one-pound bundles.

Growing to thirty feet in height, the evergreen tropical cinnamon tree has shiny, leathery leaves with yellowish-white flowers followed by dark blue berries resembling olives. The bark and leaves yield a golden oil, and the ripe fruit supplies wax for fragrant candles.

Cinnamon was one of the spices used in pharaonic Egypt during the Twentieth Dynasty, and records show that its use for medical purposes was considerable. Cinnamon was valued for its scent and antiseptic qualities, and Egyptologists have found prescriptions for cinnamon unguents to "heal every effluency, for the destruction of ulcers on gums, and to make flesh grow."

In the twelfth century, Hildegard of Bingen recommended cinnamon as a "universal spice for sinuses" and to treat colds, flu, cancer and "inner decay and slime." Cinnamon tea helps nausea and athlete's foot, and the tincture deadens the nerve in toothache. The essential is suggested for poor circulation, depression, and arthritis and muscle pain.

In aromatherapy the fragrance is thought to attract wealth.

A recipe for cinnamon cheese from biblical times calls for mixing farmer's or yogurt cheese with cinnamon and honey. In the Middle East people make a winter drink from cinnamon water and sugar. The spice is used for cooking and baking, in jellies, spiced wine and potpourri.

Meditation

Plane delayed again. Glad it's a storm, not a repair. Rather be down here anyway, Lord. Shall we look for a bookstore? It's lunchtime, too. Were you ever as hungry in Nazareth as I am right now? What did Mary prepare for you? And did the hunger grow when the cinnamon fragrance filled the air? Or was that only for holidays! Was Mary a good cook, Lord? What should be first: cinnamon roll or book?

The cinnamon temptation won out, Lord. Trouble is, now I don't have enough cash in my pocket for that book. Guess we'll be walking off the roll instead.

Nardostachys jatamansi

Spikenard

"While he was at Bethany...a woman came
with an alabaster jar of very costly ointment of nard,
and she broke open the jar and poured the ointment on his head."
—Mark 14:3

In the New Testament we read that Jesus was anointed twice with nard, or spikenard, once on his head (Mark 14:3) and once on his feet (John 12:3). In John 12:5 Judas complains that the ointment could have been sold for three hundred denarii (about fifty dollars) and the money given to the poor. But the lavish use of the ointment was in keeping with the highest form of affectionate compliment paid guests at royal feasts. This was a woman of property, able to purchase the ointment and thus show her love and gratitude to Jesus.

The ointment was extracted from the roots and young stems of *Nardostachys jatamansi,* a plant that grew at an altitude of thirteen thousand feet on the open mountainsides of Nepal, Bhutan and other parts of the Himalayas. The aromatic oil was brought to the plains of India and then carried to the Holy Land by caravan, a journey that made the nard very expensive. Some writers suggest it may have been mingled with other substances in Laodicia and Tarsus, which had the reputation of compounding the best ointments and perfumes. Pliny, Theophrastus and Dioscorides all wrote about nard, its origin and its use.

Hebrew words *nerd* and *nard* and the Greek *nardos* are translated as "spikenard." The word *nard* is derived from the Tamul, where words beginning with *nar* convey the notion of an agreeable perfume. Some commentators believe that *nardas* referred to several plants with fragrant roots and that spikenard is a kind of nard of spikelike form imported from India. The Indian name *jatamansi*, which means "a lock of hair," was given the plant by Hindu and Muslim physicians. The dried root resembles an ermine tail.

The best spikenard was imported in sealed jars of alabaster or ivory to retain the scent and stored until such time as the master of the house received distinguished guests. He would crown his guests with flowers, break the seal (not the jar) and pour out the ointment to anoint his guests. Containers for precious ointments have been found under the debris of walls and among the ruins of patrician houses. Intricately carved boxes, many made of alabaster, were found in the ruins of Nineveh.

A small plant, this perennial herb with strong and pleasantly scented roots has short spikelike stems that bear pink blossoms. It is sometimes called Indian spike. It was said to blacken the hair and promote hair growth. The ointment was used in perfumes and in medicine for the treatment of nervous disorders. Its sedative qualities helped in the treatment of epilepsy, hysteria and colic.

Both the Hebrews and the Romans used the fragrant ointment in preparing the dead for burial. Jesus refers to this practice when he says to those who scold the woman for pouring the precious ointment on his head, "[s]he has anointed my body beforehand for its burial" (Mark 14:8).

The oil is presently used to treat allergic skin reactions, rashes and tension. The fragrance is relaxing and soothing and helps nourish and regenerate the skin.

A few biblical botanists believe that the nard of the Old Testament was obtained from the flowers of lavender (*Lavandula spica*) or from camel grass (*Cymbopogon shoenanthus*). Lavender grew in the Mediterranean region, and camel grass was an important fodder grass with aromatic leaves that grew in the Arabian and northern African deserts and was also known as *nerd* and *nardos*. The references to spikenard in the Song of Solomon suggest that it was cultivated in Solomon's gardens (4:13–14).

Meditation

It was plain as day. I was jealous, Lord, raging over the unfair fine gift someone received, and all that devoted attention. It made the goosebumps crawl. I had to look away. I even turned away. The worst part was both gift giver and gift receiver noticed the repulsion in my turning. The loving moment was spoiled for them, and I was even more miserable in my isolation.

Was it something like that, Lord, when Judas spoiled the party? Was he jealous of the love poured out in gratitude to you when the precious nard was poured? And Scripture says true love is not jealous. Forgive me, Lord!

155

The Palm and the Vine

"Be bold, and bring some of the fruit of the land."
—Numbers 13:20

*T*wo of the most oft-mentioned plants in the Bible are the date palm and the grapevine. The chief food plant of the desert, the date palm was called the Tree of Life. As a symbol of Palestine the date palm symbolized victory as well as peace and plenty. The grapevine, the first cultivated plant mentioned in the Bible, also represented peace and prosperity. It is cited seventy-eight times, from the days of Noah to those of Jesus and again in Revelation. The "fruitful vine" was symbolic of the Israelites and represented the blessings of God. Later it was adopted as an emblem of the Christian church. Jesus used the vine in his teaching, comparing himself to the vine and his disciples to the branches.

Phoenix dactylifera
Date Palm

*"Then they came to E'lim, where there were twelve springs of water
and seventy palm trees...."*
—Exodus 15:27

Called *tamar* or *temarim* in Hebrew, the palm tree appears forty-two times in the Bible. This life-sustaining tree, associated with Palestine from earliest times, indicated the presence of water in the desert, provided wood and leaves for building, fruit for sustenance and materials for manuscripts. Shaped like an open umbrella, it sheltered travelers from the sun. It was often the only vegetation growing in the desert.

In Near-Eastern mythology it was identified with the Tree of Life. The Arabs said there are as many uses for date palms as there are days in the year. Paintings of palm trees are found in Egyptian tombs as early as 1405 B.C. Remnants of stone columns from Egyptian temples show capitals carved as palm trees.

Palms represented peace and plenty and were a symbol of grace and elegance for the Jews. They were a sign of majesty and fruitfulness, growing heavenward to more than eighty feet in height. The palm received its botanical name from Phoenicia, which referred to what is now Lebanon and Syria and was known as the land of palms.

The date palm takes thirty years to reach full maturity, then flourishes for a full century before beginning a gradual decline. It is said that at one time the entire Jordan valley was covered with date palm trees and that they grew over vast areas of the Holy Land. Some cities were famous for the abundance of the trees, and Jericho was called "the city of palm trees." The city of Tamar in Palestine probably received its name from the palm trees growing near it. War and drought decimated the trees, which require careful cultivation, and now they are found only along the seacoast and in desert oases.

Solomon introduced figures of palm trees into the carvings of the Temple (1 Kings 6:29, 32, 35; 7:36), and the palm tree was depicted on a Jewish coin and other ancient coins. Palms were emblems of victory or triumph. After Pompey captured Jerusalem in 63 B.C., the Romans took the palm as a symbol of their victory, and a coin commemorating the conquest of the Jews shows a woman weeping under a palm tree.

Palm fronds were carried in ceremonial processions and scattered along the way. Palm leaves and branches from other trees were used to cover the "booths" for the Feast of Tabernacles, or Sukkoth, the harvest feast, one of the "appointed festivals of the LORD" (Leviticus 23:33–44). The *lulav*, the embryonic date frond that grows in the heart of the palm, represents the time when the Israelites wandered in the desert and used all parts of the palm tree to shelter and sustain them.

> "So they took branches of palm trees and went out to meet him...."
> (John 12:13)

In the New Testament palm branches mark Jesus' triumphal entry into Jerusalem. It is said that the palm became a symbol of spiritual victory after Jesus blessed it and said, "O palm tree, may one of your branches be planted in paradise! And it shall be said of him who conquers in any contest: 'You have attained the palm of victory!'" (Gaer, *Lore of the New Testament*) This occurred after the palm tree bent its branches so Mary could pick dates when the Holy Family became hungry during the flight to Egypt. Jesus had blessed the tree and promised to return with a palm frond in his hand on Palm Sunday. Christians still carry palm branches in church on Palm Sunday to commemorate Jesus' jubilant arrival in Jerusalem.

A second-century legend tells that one morning after Mary awakened with a deep longing for her risen son, the angel Gabriel came to her and said, "Hail, Blessed Mary. Behold, I have brought unto thee a branch of the palm of Paradise." Gabriel told her that in three days she would be with Jesus and that the palm would be carried before her bier.

Later, palms were associated with martyrdom and their image was placed in Christian catacombs to mark the graves of martyrs. During the Middle Ages Christians believed that angels carried palm branches to smooth the way for martyrs on the road to heaven.

In the fourth century, when Christians reenacted the entry of Christ into Jerusalem after they had obtained religious freedom under the Roman Empire, they carried palm branches in procession and sang, "Hosannah." The custom of blessing the palms on Palm Sunday began in the eighth century.

In Sicily, palms blessed on Palm Sunday were hung in homes to bring rain and a plentiful harvest. In Austria, Bavaria and the Slavic countries, farm families walked through the fields praying and signing hymns after church on Palm Sunday, placing a sprig of palm in each pasture and barn to call God's blessing on that year's harvest.

In Arab countries every part of the palm tree is used. The wood of the palm tree is cut into planks and used in building. The leaves are woven into mats, baskets and dishes and made into brooms. They are used for thatching roofs of huts and building reed fences. The fibers provide thread and rigging for boats. Rope is made from the weblike portions of the tree's crown. The inside of the very top of the trunk is edible, tasting somewhat like celery, and heart of palm is used in salads. The sap is distilled for use in aperitifs and liqueurs. Date kernels are ground up, soaked in water and fed to livestock. Oil from the seeds is used to make soap. The date produces starch, sugar and wax. Dates are used to make wine and sweeten beer. The wine is drunk and also used to wash the body to prepare it for mummification.

The fourteenth century *Tacuinum* of Paris, an "Incunabulum of Courtly Taste," states that sweet and fresh dates are best and that they help the intestines. They are dangerous for the chest and throat, but the dangers can be neutralized with a "honeycomb," probably a suggestion that they be eaten with honey.

The date is a high-energy food because of its sugar content. It has been prescribed for asthma, chest complaints, cough and fever. It is said to help cancer of the stomach and uterus and abdominal tumors. The Arabs use the unripe fruit as an astringent for hemorrhoids, and the Lebanese say the sugar from the fruit helps hepatitis.

Meditation

Precious fruit, dried slowly, laid out open under the sun, condensing natural sweetness to delicacies for festivals— regal date for Thanksgiving bread, rich taste of health and well-being! You begin in the crown of your parent, royal palm, an origin that makes me look heavenward in the majestic fronds to find you. You grow noble, proud shade of the oasis in the desert sands, strong and firm, towering toward the heavens, yet supple enough to be humbled in the wind and bend to the fury of hurricanes.

Father, will the date and the palm teach me a lesson of greatness and humility, of festival and celebration? Can I be used to bring joy at the festival table? Can I be cut low and laid at the feet of your son? Give me such royal purpose.

Vitis vinifera

Grapevine

"If you will only heed his every commandment…
you will gather in your grain, your wine, and your oil…"
—*Deuteronomy 11:13–14*

The grapevine was one of the most important plants in the Land of Promise. It was grown in almost every part of Israel, and its fruit was an important source of energy, as either fermented wine or dried raisins.

The spies sent to the land of Canaan to scout out the territory for the Israelites returned with grapes so large that it took two men to carry a single cluster on a pole between them. They had found the grapes in the valley at Wadi Eshkol, *eshkol* meaning "grape cluster." This was the fruit of the land of milk and honey promised them by God.

Numerous references to vineyards, vinedressers and the harvest are found in the Bible.

Grapevines were often grown on slopes. They were allowed to lie on the ground during the winter and were raised on stones or stone terraces during the growing period.

> In Winter lay me down,
> In Summer raise me up.

The delicate vines were carefully pruned and tended by the vinedressers, who often lived in watchtowers in the vineyards to protect the harvest. Grapevines lie dormant during the winter, but just before Passover, new buds sprout and pale green leaves spread over the vines. The fragrance of blossoming grape flowers was so exhilarating it was given a special name, *smadar*, and mentioned in the Song of Solomon: "the vines are in blossom; they give forth fragrance" (2:13). After the dry intense heat of summer and the nourishing dew, both needed for its production, the fruit is ready for harvest, a symbol of great joy and celebration.

In Judges we read, "They went out into the field and gathered the grapes from their vineyards, trod them, and celebrated" (9:27). The harvest was the occasion for a yearly feast of joy and gladness as families came into the vineyards to gather the grapes and celebrate the bounty and blessings of God. At this time young girls selected their husbands among the youths waiting among the vines, and all would join in the singing and dancing.

Earlier, "Noah, a man of the soil, was the first to plant a vineyard. He drank some of the wine and became drunk" (Genesis 9:20–21).

The Last Supper of Jesus was a Passover meal, at which time, according to rabbinic tradition, four glasses of wine are drunk as a symbol of joy and a reminder of the four strong verbs God used in delivering the Israelites from Egypt (Exodus 6:6–7).

In Matthew 26:27–29 we read:

> Then he took a cup, and after giving thanks he gave it to them, saying, "Drink from it, all of you; for this is my blood of the covenant, which is poured out for many for the forgiveness of sins. I tell you, I will never again drink of this fruit of the vine until that day when I drink it new with you in my Father's kingdom."

Mystics who lived in sixteenth-century Safed adapted the custom of drinking four cups of wine during the Tu B'Shvat Seder and used the wine to celebrate the seasons and the changing colors of the landscape. The first cup was white, representing the first flowers of the rainy season in the fall: light-colored crocuses, narcissis and sand lilies. The second cup, white mixed with red wine, celebrated the rainy season and the white and pink cyclamens, red anemones and red Sharon tulips that bloom in November and December. The third cup, red with some white wine, recalled the month of Shvat, still winter in January and February but beginning to change: Red leaf buds appear on fig and pomegranate trees, and the pink and white buds of almond trees begin to bloom. The fourth cup was filled with red wine, celebrating Israel's spring, around the time of Pesach, or Passover, when pomegranate flowers, red buttercups and poppies bloom in the fields.

Midrashic literature, which interprets Scripture, contains many metaphors comparing the Israelites to the grapevine, so it was not surprising that Jesus used the symbol of the vine in his teaching to illustrate the idea of spiritual union: "I am the true vine, and my Father is the vinegrower. I am the vine, you are the branches" (John 15:1, 5).

Viticulture was established in Palestine in the Early Bronze Age and introduced into Egypt about 3000 B.C. Vine remains have been found at Jericho and Arad, and remains of winepresses, among the rocks of Palestine. The exact origin of the vine is unclear, but it is thought to have come from Persia. It is said that the grapevine still grows wild at the foot of Mount Ararat, in the area where Noah planted his first vineyard.

The vine appeared on the first coined money of Jewish princes, as a single leaf, a branch or a cluster of grapes. From old manuscripts we know that a vine sculpted from gold, bearing clusters of fruit made of precious stones, once adorned the east wall of the great Temple of Jerusalem. The golden vine, symbol of the Jewish nation, was carried to Rome after Vespasian and Titus conquered the city and destroyed the Temple in A.D. 70.

The Hebrew is *gefen* or *gephen* for "vine"; *kerem* for "vineyard"; and *anavim* for "grape."

There are almost as many medicinal uses for products of the vine as there are references to it in the Bible. Wine was used as an anesthetic and to reduce the anguish of capital punishment. Mixed with other ingredients it was used as a laxative and to stimulate the appetite, kill worms, ease pain and cure coughs. It was a folk remedy for rheumatism, and the sap of young branches was used as a remedy for skin diseases.

Grape leaves are astringent and were used for diarrhea; juice of unripe fruit, also astringent, was used for throat infections. The leaves are said to be rich in an antiarthritic, anticancer and anticardiac compound.

Raisins taken with figs were used as a laxative. They were said to be pain relieving and anti-inflammatory and to ease arthritic pain, gout and migraines.

In cooking, grape leaves were used in soups, stews and stir-fry dishes. Stuffed grape leaves, leaves wrapped around rice or meat and cooked, are still a delicacy in some cultures. Grape honey, made like sugarless jams and jellies, was added to yogurt for a sweetened drink.

Meditation

There are wild grapevines growing at the fence line, Lord! Plucked their fruit and winced, spitting out the seeds and skin. A teacher long ago taught us how to prepare wild grapes for jelly. Such a lot of work and much too busy to be bothered now. Is it true, Lord, that people got in tubs of grapes and pressed out the juice barefoot? You would know. You might have made the tubs.

And wine. I've traveled down the Rhine and Moselle many times, Lord. The vineyards are remarkable tucked among the rock. The connoisseurs, so I've been told, can tell blindfolded from which vineyard on the river bends a certain wine comes.

When all is said and done about grapes—from jelly to foot stomping to finest vintage—one thing is left that matters, and I thank you, Lord. You took this common, wonderful thing to be your memory, to be your blood— crushed and shared.

Tithing Herbs

"All tithes from the land, whether the seed from the ground
or the fruit from the tree, are the LORD's...
All tithes of herd and flock, every tenth one that passes under the shepherd's staff,
shall be holy to the LORD.
These are the commandments that the LORD gave to Moses
for the people of Israel on Mount Sinai."
—Leviticus 27:30–32, 34

$\mathcal{M}$osaic law required that the Jews pay a tithe, or one tenth, of their crops or profits justly acquired to the priests of the temple for their support or for religious and charitable uses. This included all crops, including fruit, and stock. Every third year the tithes were brought to town so that the "Levites, because they have no allotment or inheritance with you, as well as the resident aliens, the orphans, and the widows...may come and eat their fill" (Deuteronomy 14:29).

The Bible mentions four herbs in connection with tithing: mint, dill, cumin and rue. These herbs were simple and inexpensive, cultivated but also growing wild, and of relatively little importance, even though they were used extensively for cooking and medicinal purposes.

Jesus' warning to the scribes and Pharisees—that while they are following the letter of the law, they are neglecting the spirit of the law—is thus even more condemning. Not only do they give of their goods and not from their hearts but the goods they give are of little monetary value.

Anethum graveolens

Anise, Dill

"Woe to you, scribes and Pharisees, hypocrites!
For you tithe mint, dill, and cummin,
and have neglected the weightier matters of the law:
justice and mercy and faith.
It is these you ought to have practiced without neglecting the others."
—*Matthew 23:23*

The word *anethum,* which occurs only in Matthew 23:23, has been translated by some as "anise." However the plant referred to in this passage is now thought to be dill, *Anethum graveolens.* Anise was in great repute among the ancient Assyrians, according to clay tablets from the library at Nineveh. True anise, *Pimpinella anisum,* has properties similar to dill.

Dill was one of the earliest-known herbs of the ancient world. The earliest record of the herb appears on Egyptian papyrus from 3000 B.C. Dill was an ancient Egyptian remedy. In the Ebers papyrus of about 1500 B.C., dill is included as an ingredient in a pain-killing mixture. In Greece its use was well established by the time of Aristotle (fourth century B.C.). The ancient Greeks covered their eyes with fronds of dill to induce sleep. The second-century Greek physician Galen wrote: "Dill procureth sleep, wherefore garlands of Dill are worn at feasts."

Dioscorides and Pliny also knew the herb, and the Romans wore wreaths of dill at their feasts. The Roman poet Virgil wrote of the herb's fragrance:

Et florem jungit bene olentis anethi.
And adds the flower of the fragrant dill.

The name *dill* derives from the old Norse word *dylla*, meaning "to dill" or "soothe," and refers to the plant's ability to soothe "gripes"—colic or intestinal spasms. The Saxon word *dili* meant "to lull."

Dill-water, or "gripe-water" has been used for lulling babies to sleep for centuries. The words "dilly, dilly" in this old lullaby may be a reference to dill water having been given to a restless baby.

Lavender's blue, dilly, dilly,
Lavender's green,
When you are king, dilly, dilly,
I shall be queen. (Gordon, *Green Magic*)

In 1305 dill was one of the drugs taxed in England for ships reaching London Bridge as they approached the city. Edward I of England needed money to repair the bridge so this "highly-prized herb" was taxed.

The Talmud states that dill's seeds, stems and leaves were subject to tithe. Dill is native to the Mediterranean and Black Sea regions. It grew wild in biblical times but was also cultivated in gardens. It still grows wild in Palestine, especially on the plain of Sharon and near Nazareth. It grows along riverbanks and wadis and in various other habitats.

Leaves of the fragrant dill were used as a marinating spice, in sour condiments and in seasoning cakes. The aromatic plant resembles fennel. Dill's finely divided leaves, called dill weed, are used in soups and to spice beets and pickles. Dill weed loses its flavor when cooked or dried, so the fresh leaves are added to foods just before they are served.

Eating the leaves is said to increase mental vitality and clear focus. The seeds retain their flavor and can be chewed to freshen the breath. Dill water made from the seeds is used for colic and other gastric upsets. The Copts used it as a mouth rinse. Dill seeds steeped in hot milk will quiet the nerves; in Holland this mixture is used to induce sleep. Dill tea will help hiccups, upset stomach and insomnia.

In early American days dill seeds, called "meeting seeds" and "meeting house seeds," were chewed during long church services to prevent sleep and to quiet rumbling stomachs.

Meditation

To discover usefulness in all things means to discover the gift therein given. It behooves the receiver to take pleasure in the gift, to use it according to its created and given intent—to govern its use thoughtfully.

Lord, you have commanded that proper governance includes returning to you at least a tenth of the gift's fruitfulness. My stingy heart asks why—you have no need of your gifts returned. Or do you?

We are not to neglect justice, mercy, faith. Is not the sharing of things—be they as small and insignificant as seeds of anise and dill—an act of justice, mercy and love of God? Break away, Lord, the prison of my stinginess.

Cuminum cyminum

Cumin

"Dill is not threshed with a threshing sledge,
nor is a cart wheel rolled over cummin;
but dill is beaten out with a stick,
and cummin with a rod."

—Isaiah 28:27

Cumin was an important herb for the Hebrews, who used it to stem bleeding following circumcision. The small, round grains are the fruit of the plant, easily bruised if not properly gathered. A slight shake of the stalks dislodges the fruit; rough handling could crush the grain and release the oil.

Isaiah tells us that cumin and dill are carefully harvested and that God's loving-kindness extends to his people, just as the farmer treats each crop with care. God deals differently with different people just as the farmer uses different methods in threshing such crops as dill, cumin, wheat and barley.

The ancient Greeks referred to mean and stingy persons as "cumin splitters," a reference to the minute seeds, and the Romans nicknamed Marcus Aurelius a "cumin splitter" because of his avarice. Native to the Mediterranean region, cumin was used by the Minoans in the thirteenth century B.C. Cumin grains have been found in the tombs of the pharaohs of the Eighteenth Dynasty, around 1539 B.C., and in the Tomb of Kha at Dei el-Medina, but not

TITHING HERBS

in archaeological excavations in Israel. During the Twentieth Dynasty cumin was one of the offerings Ramses III presented to the temple of Re at Heliopolis.

Egyptian medical texts from the Eighteenth Dynasty reveal considerable use of cumin, called *tepnen*, for stomach ailments, head illness, skin ailments and abscesses. The Ebers papyrus mentions cumin in nine medical recipes, including one for intestinal parasites. A prescription for an unguent to ease headaches included cumin, myrrh, lotus flowers, juniper berries, moringa tree oil and two unidentified ingredients. *The Assyrian Herbal* recommends cumin for eye poultices and insect stings.

Cumin contains pain-relieving compounds and has many anti-inflammatory properties. In modern herbal medicine it is still used to treat digestive problems. Cumin supports and stimulates the immune system and may help poor circulation. In aromatherapy the essential oil is said to increase the appetite. Cumin has been used in Palestine to treat cattle with ulcers from insect bites and worms deposited in the skin by flies.

The Roman author Pliny extolled the virtues of Egyptian cumin: "Of all the seasonings which gratify a fastidious taste cumin is the most agreeable." He wrote that Alexandrian bread was flavored with cumin. A recipe for Alexandrian sauce for grilled fish in Marcus Apicius's first-century Roman cookbook called for cumin, lovage, oregano, celery seed, vinegar, oil and four other ingredients.

During times of ceremonial and penitential fasting, cumin was a welcome flavoring for bread and other dishes, enhancing the flavor of bland food and helping compensate for the lack of meat. In the days of the Jewish kingdom in Palestine, it was customary to proclaim a fast day in times of drought, plague or famine. National days of mourning and fasting were ordained following the destruction of the first Temple in 586 B.C.

As in biblical times, cumin today is crushed and ground and added to bread dough and stews. The grains are an ingredient in curry powder and flavor cheese, chutney, meat, pickles and sausage. The oil is used in perfumes and liqueurs.

An annual herb, the cumin plant is not found wild, except for a hairy variety from Turkestan. It grows to two feet in height and produces clusters of dainty white or rose flowers and hairy fruits.

Kammon, a village near Acre, is said to be named after the Hebrew word for *cumin* and for the sharp smell in the area.

Meditation

Rushing out to work I crushed the empty bun package to trash it. Yellow-brown bitsy seeds stuck on my hand. What a shame, Lord, I thought. They're my favorite part. And like so often before, I wondered about the hands that harvested the cumin somewhere unknown to me, and I asked you to bless those hands.

And, Lord, I wondered whose hands long ago harvested cumin to heal your circumcision. Yellow-brown bitsy seeds, rich in oil and taste, gently harvested; seed preserved and planted year after year. Seed tithed for healing, tithed for fragrance. Way back then who pressed out cumin's essence for the first time to make fragrance to delight the senses?

Let there be no haste, no waste, in even the tiniest thing. The cumin tithed me a bit of joy today, Lord. How can I tithe the joy further?

Mentha longifolia

Mint

(Horsemint)

"But woe to you Pharisees!
For you tithe mint and rue and herbs of all kinds,
and neglect justice and the love of God..."
—Luke 11:42

The Pharisee taxed himself lightly if he paid the tithe of mint, for it was too common and too easily cultivated to be of much worth, even though it was valuable as a medicinal herb. It was one of the plants subject to the ban on sowing and gathering every seventh year. Jesus' lesson in hypocrisy is told by Matthew and again by Luke, and mint is the one herb mentioned by both.

The Greek word *Heduosmos*, or *mintha*, means "having a sweet smell" and refs to "a sweet smelling herb or mint." The plant derives its name from Mintha, a Greek nymph who was transformed into the herb by Persephone after Persephone learned that her husband, Pluto, had loved the nymph.

During the Middle Ages all mints were dedicated to the Virgin Mary. In England, John Gerard called mint Our Lady's Mint. It was called *Herba Santa Maria* in Italy and *Menthe de Notre Dame* in France. *Mentha spicata* is called Mary's Mint, and *Mentha arvensis* is Our Lady's Plant. Mint and other Mary-named herbs and flowers were planted in medieval paradise gardens.

Several varieties of mint grew in Israel, but horsemint is the most common and probably the one referred to by Matthew and Luke. Horsemint is still found today in the Holy Land and is cultivated at Aleppo in Syria. It is much larger than the other mints, reaching a height of three feet or more, with lilac flowers. It grows in moist, sunny places where it tends to run wild. It has been confused with *Mentha spicata,* or spearmint.

The Egyptians recognized the medicinal value of this ancient Chinese plant as early as 1550 B.C. Mint was cultivated in Egyptian gardens and is mentioned in Egyptian and Assyrian medical texts from the time. It was used in poultices for eye, ear and mouth ailments and for itchy feet. Internally it helped bad breath, heartburn and urinary problems and served as an enema. Part of a bouquet that included leaves of peppermint was found in a tomb dating from the Late Period (715–332 B.C.) in Egypt. Dioscorides gives the Egyptian name of the plant as *tis* and said it was used as a tonic for the stomach.

Prospero Alpini, who wrote about ancient Egyptian medicine, said that a warm decoction of mint was administered to a patient to treat fever.

The Greeks and Romans learned of mint from the Hebrews, who brought it to Palestine. The first-century Roman author Pliny, author of *Naturalis Historia,* listed forty-one remedies in which mint was thought to be helpful. The Romans used it in "many kinds of pottage and to boil with pulse and other things, to impart sweetness to their flavor." The Greeks used it in the bath to strengthen "the nerves and sinews" of athletes, and even today it is added to hot baths to treat skin ailments.

The Hebrews used mint as a strewing herb at home and in the Temple, prizing its clean and aromatic scent. They served mint at the Spring Feast of the Paschal Lamb, and today it is one of the "bitter herbs" of the paschal feast. A yogurt drink from biblical times is made with diluted yogurt, six sprigs of chopped and crushed fresh mint and salt or honey for seasoning.

Greek and Roman physicians suggested hanging mint in sick rooms to speed healing. In aromatherapy spearmint promotes healing and brings about a feeling of balance and a sense of well-being.

Marcus Apicius, Roman epicure from the first century, used green and preserved mint as a condiment on almost every page of his cookbook. Mint sauce was served with lamb and other meat dishes. Mint was used to flavor stuffings for vegetables and mixed with yogurt for a summer salad dressing. Mint boiled with vinegar and sugar, cooled and diluted with cold water, made a refreshing drink.

Mint tea helps improve digestion and settle the stomach. Mint is used as a stimulant and is said to help headaches and general pain. Used in potpourri or sachets, mint will repel clothes moths. It is said to keep ants away from the house.

Meditation

There's a patch of mint by the back door. It crowds out everything else, but that's okay. When I walk past I snip a leaf and rub it for the fragrance. Rather detest mint candies, but have made many a cup of tea with its fresh greens. Now, mint jelly is its own story. First time I had mint jelly was at Mary Kay's on Holy Thursday after your Last Supper service, Lord. She invited us up for a Seder meal. She had all the makings— the lamb chops, the bitter herbs and all the trimmings. I was to bring mint jelly.

Well, Lord, you know I don't like mint jelly at all, but it was just the right thing! It was delicious with the lamb. But I remember more that evening: a common bond shared around a cramped apartment table, eight people with next to nothing in common—except you and the lamb and the readings of the ancients and fine conversation and mint jelly.

Lord, the rest of that mint jelly sat for a couple of years in my fridge. It needed lamb and company to go with it, it needed the wisdom of the ancients and it needed Mary Kay.

TITHING HERBS

Ruta graveolens

Rue

*"Set apart a tithe of all the yield of your seed
that is brought in yearly from the field."*
—Deuteronomy 14:22

Regulations concerning tithes spelled out in Deuteronomy also required that "those who have no allotment or inheritance, as well as the resident aliens, the orphans and the widows," be invited to come and eat their fill at the yearly tithing. Those who feared the Lord God were told, "do not be hard-hearted or tight-fisted toward your needy neighbor...give liberally and be ungrudging when you do so."

According to Talmudic law rue was not subject to tithe because it was not regularly cultivated in gardens. But in Jesus' time it was grown in gardens and thus subject to tithe. The Pharisees followed the letter of the law, tithing rue as required. Jesus reminds them that they "neglected the weightier matters of the law: justice and mercy and faith" (Matthew 23:23).

Heavily scented, with bitter-tasting leaves that can cause a severe rash when touched, rue was widely regarded in biblical times as a medicinal panacea.

The ancient Greeks called rue *peganon*, which means "to save" or "to release," and used it as a preventive and antidote for poisons. Perhaps because of its strong odor, the Greeks believed rue prevented contagion and disease. "It drives away the plague if you merely smell of it." The botanist Theophrastus and physician Dioscorides, both ancient herbalists, knew the value of rue, and it was prescribed in *The Assyrian Herbal,* a compilation of plant lists and medical texts dating to the end of the second millennium B.C.

Prospero Alpini said the Egyptians of his day used the oil for massage for feverish conditions "like the ancients did it." In first-century Rome, Pliny recommended honeyed wine flavored with rue and said that rue was considered effectual for eighty-four maladies.

An eye lotion made from rue was used to restore failing eyesight and preserve vision. Rue treated epilepsy and snake and insect bites and was also used externally for skin diseases and rheumatism. In folk medicine the juice was applied for earaches and was an ingredient in bitters, an aromatic appetite stimulant. Italians ate the leaves in salads to preserve eyesight.

Rue and garlic were among the ingredients of the noted "vinegar of the four thieves," used by four anonymous villains for protection against infection when they broke into homes during the plague of Marseilles in the sixteenth century.

The botanical name aptly describes rue. In Latin *ruta* means "bitterness" or "unpleasantness" and *graveolen,* "heavy-scented." The word *rue* derives from the Old English *hreowan,* "to make penitent, to distress," and one of its earliest meanings was "sorrow" or "regret." In English folklore and literature rue was a symbol of grief, repentance and bitterness. Shakespeare called it the "sour herb of grace."

Christian missionaries to the ancient Britons sprinkled holy water with branches of rue, showering the congregation before and after a service. It may have been used by the early Catholic church to repel demons and evil because rue was thought to kill fleas and repel insects. Later, bunches of rue were used to sprinkle the faithful before High Mass, perhaps because of its association with grace and repentance.

A hardy evergreen dwarf shrub, rue grows on the hillsides and in the *bathah,* or thickets, in Palestine. The Swedish naturalist Hasselquist saw it growing wild on Mount Tabor. Rue is grown in gardens for its delicate blue-green leaves, small yellow flowers and heavy scent.

Flavius Josephus, who wrote about Jewish life in the first century, mentions a special kind of rue in his description of the fortress of Machaerus, situated at the northeastern end of the Dead Sea: "Within the palace once grew a plant of rue, of an amazing size; indeed, in height and thickness no fig-tree surpassed it. Tradition said that it had lasted from the time of Herod."

Fresh or dried leaves are used sparingly to season cheese, vegetable juice, salads, stews and vegetables. Rue loses its aroma but not its taste when dried. Rue is considered medicinally safe if picked in the early morning but poisonous if gathered later, after the sun has influenced it.

Ruta is a homeopathic remedy prescribed for eyestrain, sprains and injuries to bones, sciatica, backache and dental problems. It is considered a calming influence in aromatherapy.

Meditation

Little rue, I don't know you! I've only just learned about you but have no experience of touching or tasting you or inhaling the scent of your blossoms. So now my journey begins, for I must hunt you down and experience you to know how to relate to you. I only know what I read here and am intrigued by it to search for you and your healing.

And so the credit of love and faith goes to the depicters in word and image who aid this encounter with you through this volume.

Lord, so it is and so it ends—only to begin again—the search for the Father's gifts and the Spirit that kindles gratitude for them in our hearts, everywhere, at all times, in every person, place and event. When I bump into rue, or you, will I recognize either of you? And will I have learned a little to tithe, to return your love to you and to the land and to my neighbor? How else shall your providence be recognized and praised!

PART FOUR

Scripture Gardens

"And the Lord God planted a garden in Eden, in the east;
and there he put the man whom he had formed.
Out of the ground the Lord God made to grow every tree
that is pleasant to the sight and good for food…."
—*Genesis 2:8–9*

*O*n the first book of the Bible, we read that on the third day God planted a garden. He filled it with "vegetation: plants yielding seed of every kind, and trees of every kind bearing fruit with the seed in it" (Genesis 1:12). Many gardens are mentioned in the Bible, the Garden of Eden being the first. Gardens are where significant events of the Bible occur: the temptation and fall of man in the Garden of Eden, the agony of Christ in the Garden of Gethsemane and Christ's resurrection in the garden of Joseph of Arimathea. Jesus taught in gardens, using fruit and vine to illustrate his message. Jesus prayed in an olive garden—the Mount of Olives.

Scriptures describe lavish gardens. King Solomon, perhaps the first botanist, had a garden filled with fruit and nut trees, flowering and aromatic shrubs, sweet-scented herbs, exotic spice plants and pools of water for irrigation. The Song of Solomon is set in a garden filled with choice fruits and fragrant spices. The king's garden in the City of David embodied the pool of Shelah (Nehemiah 3:15).

A healing garden is described in the final book of the Bible. John's vision of the new Jerusalem includes on "either side of the river…the tree of life with its twelve kinds of fruit, producing its fruit each month; and the leaves of the tree are for the healing of the nations" (Revelation 22:2).

In biblical times people knew of the healing power of certain plants and trees. During the Middle Ages this knowledge became suspect and was considered pagan. Much of it was lost, but the monks kept alive herbal traditions and lore, growing plants in their monastery gardens and using them for healing. During the Renaissance, physicians became interested in medicinal plants, believing that plants were on this earth for our benefit and every plant had a function: If it could not be eaten, it must be medicinal. They grew plants in physic gardens in order to study them.

Today physic gardens and herb gardens are established so we can learn about medicinal plants. Biblical plants are prominent in these gardens. Trees and shrubs mentioned in the Bible grow in biblical gardens of all sizes, with biblical references on signs and plaques to connect the plant with Scripture. These gardens provide inspiration, encourage prayer and meditation and educate visitors about biblical life and events.

Gardens to Visit

There are biblical gardens throughout the world, many in the United States, some in Canada, England and Scotland, and some in the Holy Land. They are associated with churches and synagogues, botanical gardens and conservatories, or they are under private auspices. They may be part of a large herb garden, and some gardens, not specifically Bible gardens, contain a large number of biblical plants. Some also contain plants with modern biblical associations, such as Jacob's ladder, or that grew in biblical times, such as the chaste tree.

Some biblical gardens are in Quiet Gardens, part of the Quiet Garden Trust, a ministry of hospitality and prayer that began at Stoke Poges, Buckinghamshire, England, in 1992. Quiet Gardens are associated with retreat centers, churches and private homes and offer planned periods of prayer, silence, reflection, spiritual refreshment and support.

The gardens described below are either biblical gardens or gardens where many biblical plants grow. As plans and plants in gardens change over the years, some gardens lose their biblical focus and new biblical gardens emerge. Information about them can be found on such Web sites as www.biblicalgardens.com and www.sover.net/hkfamily. The wise visitor will call before making a trip to a distant garden.

United States

CALIFORNIA

Bible Garden
Congregation B'nai Shalom
74 Eckley Ln.
Walnut Creek, CA 94596
Phone: 925-934-9446
E-mail: office@bshalom.org
Open daily

Biblical trees and plants, planted within the last ten years, surround the synagogue. Rockrose, rosemary, wormwood and dwarf oleander bloom along the street in front of the parking area. Large palm trees, laden with clusters of dates, line the path to the sanctuary and tulips and narcissus bloom there in the spring. Flowering crabapple, locust, fig, oak and palm trees grow along the Golden Path, leading to the social hall. Lavender, daisies, thistle, bay laurel, myrtle and juniper grow here. Behind the sanctuary, grape-bearing vines cover the pergola of the Sukkoth booth. An almond tree and willows join crepe myrtle and juniper, more oleander and date palms in another area.

Biblical Botanical Garden
Garden Church
8712 E. Santa Ana Canyon Rd.
Anaheim Hills, CA 92808
Phone: 714-282-1899
E-mail: BCrow87044@aol.com
Open daily

Located on sixty-seven acres in southern California in a climate similar to that of the Holy Land, the Biblical Botanical Garden has a Garden of Gethsemane with an olive grove of 115 trees, many of the fruit trees of the Bible, an oak tree similar to the Israel type, palm and cedar trees and many bushes and flowers. The garden has been developing since 1997, and focal points already completed include the Hill of the Cross and a reflection pond shaped like the Sea of Galilee. Yet to be completed are the Jordan River, first-century aqueduct and Garden Tomb sites.

Biblical Garden
Strybing Arboretum and Botanical Gardens
Golden Gate Park

Ninth Ave. at Lincoln Way

San Francisco, CA 94122

Phone: 415-661-1316

Web site: www.strybing.org

Open daily

A sunny, sheltered corner of the arboretum cradles the biblical garden, half-circled by the fragrance garden, which also contains biblical plants. Sunrose and rockrose plants form a multicolored ground cover for the main bed of the biblical garden, dedicated in 1975. Rosemary, juniper, fig and tamarisk grow here. A large sweep of lavender on the right marks the entrance to the pathway. Sage grows to the left along the top of the limestone wall. Other culinary herbs found along the wall are thyme, dill and hyssop. Alliums and cumin grow here. Further along is the final bed, with pomegranate, etrog (citrus), grapevines, acanthus and styrax growing together with sorrel, acanthus, myrtle and flowering or manna ash.

The Master's Garden, Church of the Wayfarer
Carmel, CA

The Master's Garden
Church of the Wayfarer
Lincoln St. and Seventh Ave.
PO Box 2205
Carmel, CA 93921
Phone: 831-624-3550
E-mail: WayfarerChurch@aol.com
Open daily

This one-hundred-year-old terraced garden running along the front of this United Methodist church on Lincoln Street in the picturesque downtown area of Carmel-by-the-Sea was designed to attract and add happiness to all who pass by. A very old cedar of Lebanon tree grows near the entrance. A statue of Saint Francis nestled below the branches of a native manzanita tree in a corner nook greets visitors. An open book proclaims "Bible Garden," and an archway leads to two paths, an upper one on the right, a lower one to the left. Biblical flowers and herbs line the walks and lead to the Seventh Street side, where acanthus, bay laurel, and old fig, olive and cypress trees grow. A fountain, steeplelike sculpture and wooden altar further define the spiritual intent of the garden.

Meditation/Memorial Garden
St. Bonaventure Catholic Church
5562 Clayton Rd.
Concord, CA 94521
Phone: 925-672-5800
Open daily

Covering approximately one-half acre to the side and behind the church, the garden is intended to encourage meditation and reflection on the Bible, God, Jesus and Mary. Stations of the Cross and statues of Mary and Jesus encourage this, as do benches placed along winding paths that cross three footbridges. Blossoms and leaves of poppies, lavender, sage and other biblical flora carpet the area. Irises and lilies grow along a landscaped streambed, and cascading rosemary bushes cover naturalized mounds. Pomegranate, myrtle and sycamore trees mingle with the chaste tree and native redwoods in the garden, begun in 1986. A memorial garden with more than a hundred rose bushes and trees is behind the church.

Memorial Biblical Garden
Episcopal Church of the Epiphany
5450 Churchwood Dr.
Oak Park, CA 91377
Phone: 818-991-4797
E-mail: helens@pacificnet.net
Open daily

Designed in the shape of a cross, the Memorial Biblical Garden has a fountain at its center, symbolizing the waters that God created to feed the life he created on earth. A bay laurel tree grows in the center of the herb garden that contains hyssop, coriander, thyme, rue, dill and other biblical herbs. Apricot, fig, pomegranate, olive and acacia trees are here, as are juniper, myrtle and wormwood. Dedicated in 1994, the garden is already expanding, with a mini-vineyard on the hillside above.

COLORADO

Scripture Garden
Denver Botanic Gardens
1005 York St.
Denver, CO 80206
Phone: 720-865-3500
Web site: www.botanicgardens.org
Open daily

The Scripture Garden, completed in 1981, brings to mind the Holy Land with its use of sandstone for raised beds, benches, pathways and pool. The striking bronze and mosaic sculpture in the center depicts symbols of Jewish and Christian faiths. The garden incorporates many plants of the biblical age, among them pomegranate, date palm, fig, grape, olive, apricot, cedar of Lebanon, bay, oak, myrtle, papyrus and rushes. Lentils, fava beans and vegetables and herbs from that period are also in the garden.

A sign at the garden's entrance reminds visitors that sacred writings of many religions contain references to plants, and invites them to share favorite passages or sacred thoughts in a weatherproof book.

The Oak Park Conservatory

615 Garfield St.
Oak Park, IL 60304
Phone: 708-386-4700
Web site: www.oprf.com/conservatory
Open daily

A small biblical garden at the west wall in the Desert House includes several varieties of papyrus, pomegranate, laurel, olive, fig and etrog (citron) trees, and large myrtle and rosemary bushes. Four kinds of medicinal aloe grow in another section of the Desert House. A pomegranate tree is also found in the Fern House. Begun as a community effort in 1914 with plants brought back from foreign places by residents, the conservatory is now the third largest in the Chicago area.

INDIANA

Warsaw Biblical Gardens

313 S. Buffalo St.
Warsaw, IN 46580
Phone: 219-267-6419
Web site: www.warsawbiblicalgardens.org
Open May 15 through September 15

Six microclimates represent the main Bible environments in this compact garden of just under one acre located thirty-six miles west of Fort Wayne. A walk through the gardens takes the visitor through a desert where tamarisk and broom grow, past a brook flanked by such biblical lilies as yellow flag iris and hyacinth and through a forest with woodland plants. The orchard contains fig, pomegranate, apple and other fruit trees. Grapevines cover a large arbor, and the meadow in the center of the garden is home to many "flowers of the field." More than one hundred species grow in the gardens that also include an herb and crop area. Here bitter herbs, tithing herbs and fragrant herbs grow, along with melons, hyssop, wheat, barley and various legumes.

FLORIDA

The Garden of Our Lord
St. James Lutheran Church
110 Phoenetia Ave.
Coral Gables, FL 33134
Phone: 305-443-0014
Open daily

A magnificent almond tree stretches its sheltering arms over the entrance to this walled garden, and spreading date palms and olive trees, fig trees and pomegranates greet the visitor. Winding paths lead past myrtle and spikenard, frankincense, cassia, aloe and carob bushes and trees. Sycamore, cypress and mulberry trees are represented. Willows and bulrushes nod beside the Children's Pool where lotus blooms. Above the pool a marble figure of Christ, with arm raised in benediction, rises over a handmade hill built of coral rock and soil. Diagonally across the garden rises a seven-foot wrought iron cross. All of the plants in this garden, begun in 1945 and continuously augmented, derive from the Holy Land.

MASSACHUSETTS

Biblical Garden
Episcopal Church of the Holy Spirit
204 Monument Rd.
Orleans, MA 02653
Phone: 508-255-0433
E-mail: morgnway@capecod.net
Open daily

More than forty biblical flowers, shrubs and trees grow in this recently expanded 280-square-foot garden that borders two sides of a small building on the church property. A fig tree marks the entrance and hazelnut, quince and a bay tree also grow here. Herbs include rue, sage, hyssop, mint, parsley and sorrel. The lilies of the field—anemone, lily, iris and narcissus—are represented. The fig tree and other tender plants spend the winter in the greenhouse, and the garden is replanted in late April.

MISSOURI

Biblical Garden
Missouri Botanical Garden
4344 Shaw Blvd.
St. Louis, MO 63166
Phone: 800-642-8842
Web site: www.mobot.org
Open daily except Christmas Day

Biblical plants are found not only in the biblical garden but also in several of the other gardens in the Shoenberg Temperate House, which displays plants unique to the Mediterranean and other temperate regions of the world. The biblical garden features thirty to forty plants mentioned in the Bible, including date palm and pomegranate trees, grapes, capers, henna, wheat and sorghum. Olive, carob and bay laurel grow in an upstairs garden, and figs ripen on the large fig tree in the Moorish Garden.

NEW YORK

Biblical Garden
Cathedral Church of St. John the Divine
1047 Amsterdam Ave. at 112th St.
New York, NY 10025
Phone: 212-316-7540
Web site: www.stjohndivine.org
Open daily

Enclosed by fieldstone walls and the southeast wall of the cathedral, the sixteen-hundred-square-foot garden was redesigned in 2001. Every herb, plant, flower, tree and shrub that grows there is related to plants in existence in the Holy Land two thousand or more years ago and mentioned in Scripture. Visitors entering through a new wooden lych-gate, a roofed portal common to churchyards, are greeted with a profusion of plants that includes crocus, iris, sage, thistle, lily, almond, cedar of Lebanon, juniper, Mediterranean Cypress, pine and plum. A bluestone walk in the shape of a cross bisects the garden. At its center are a twelve-foot-diameter ceramic motif patterned after the cathedral's Great Rose window and a low fountain with gently bubbling water. Four dwarf palms in wooden planters grace this pivotal area. A secluded place to rest or meditate, the garden was a gift of Sarah Larkin Loening in 1972 and was previously restored in 1988.

Biblical Garden in the Lowe Herb Garden

Nannen Arboretum
28 Parkside Dr.
Ellicottville, NY 14731
Phone: 716-699-2377 ext. 128
Open daily

A number of biblical herbs grow in the twelve specialty gardens in the eighty-eight-hundred-square-foot herb garden, donated by the S. Arthur Lowe family and dedicated in 1984. In the biblical garden, an area of approximately sixty square feet, are aloe, hyssop, rue, spices that include cumin and coriander, flax, Egyptian onion, wormwood, Madonna lily and other biblical plants. Onions, chives and dill, marjoram, sage, thyme and other biblical herbs grow in the culinary garden. Mints and oregano are found in the beverage garden. Many of the biblical herbs grow in the medicinal garden and the Dioscorides medicinal garden that also has globe thistle and daisies.

Thyme bench, Medieval Garden, Cox Arboretum, Dayton, OH

Biblical Garden

Cox Arboretum Gardens
6733 Springboro Pike
Dayton, OH 45449
Phone: 937-434-9005
Web site: www.metroparks.org
Open daily except Christmas Day and New Year's Day

A young chaste tree blooms among Balm of Gilead, milk thistle, hyssop, cumin, myrtle and wormwood in the biblical garden area of the Thyme in Paradise medieval garden. More biblical plants are found in the medicinal bed, where mint, sweet flag and blue flag, rosemary and the oak of Jerusalem flourish. Sage, parsley, marjoram, chives and other biblical herbs are in the culinary plot, and flax grows in the housewife's garden. A vine-covered wattle fence surrounds the paradise garden, shaped like a stained-glass window.

Bible Garden

Inniswood Metro Gardens
940 S. Hempstead Rd.
Westerville, OH 43081
Phone: 614-895-6216
Web site: www.metroparks.net/inniswood.htm
Open daily

The Bible garden is only one of the several rooms in the Herb Garden that contain biblical plants and herbs. Rosemary topiaries, cedars of Lebanon, date palm, pomegranate, olive, bay laurel, fig and carob trees spend their summers in pots in the biblical garden and winters in the greenhouses. A hand-hewn sandstone watering trough from the 1880s anchors one end of the garden, and a grapevine-covered pergola is opposite. Madonna lilies, narcissis and irises bloom here, as do a chaste tree and an apricot tree. Thyme, rue, leeks, coriander, mint and sage culinary herbs abound. Winding paths lead to the medicinal, culinary and thyme collections that also contain biblical plants. The Herb Garden, dedicated in 1988, is maintained by the Herb Society of America, Central Ohio Unit.

Biblical Botanical Garden

Rodef Shalom

4905 Fifth Ave.

Pittsburgh, PA 15213

Phone: 412-621-6566

Web site: www.rodefshalom.org/Garden

Open June 1 through September 15:

Sunday through Thursday 10 a.m.–2 p.m.;

Wednesday 10 a.m.–2 p.m. and 7–9 p.m.;

Friday closed; Saturday noon–1 p.m.

A cascading waterfall, a desert and a bubbling stream representing the Jordan River meandering from Lake Kinneret to the Dead Sea highlight this garden, designed to represent the land of the Bible. More than one hundred temperate and tropical plants of the Bible are found in this one-third-acre garden. Papyrus and rushes grow along the stream. Lotus and water lilies bloom in the Lake Kinneret pond. Olive, date, pomegranate, fig, cedar, cypress, tamarisk, sycamore and other trees mentioned in the Bible are found here. A grape arbor shades a meandering path, and local plants with biblical names thrive alongside biblical herbs and flowers. Plant displays and programs on such themes as botanical symbols in world religions, drugs and pharmaceuticals in the early biblical world and fragrance through the ages are presented each season.

Water lilies bloom in Lake Kinneret pond,
Biblical Botanical Garden, Rodef Shalom, Pittsburg, PA

Biblical Garden
Temple Beth-El
70 Orchard Ave.
Providence, RI 02906
Phone: 401-331-6070
E-mail: RShalansky@temple-beth-el.org
Open Sunday through Thursday

Branches of a weeping mulberry tree frame the stone tablets of the Ten Commandments that symbolize the central theme of this garden. Apricot and tamarisk trees, underplanted with sage, crocus and wormwood, anchor each end of the long narrow garden. Rue, juniper and anemone grow here amid the myrtle and narcissus ground cover. The biblical garden of the upper garden of the temple, dedicated in 1960, was refurbished in 2001.

SOUTH CAROLINA

Biblical Garden
Magnolia Plantations and Its Gardens
3550 Ashley River Rd.
Charleston, SC 29414
Phone: 843-571-1266; 800-367-3517
Web site: www.magnoliaplantation.com/gardens
Open daily 8 a.m.–5 p.m. EST (call for November through February hours)

Herbs and plants of the New Testament surround a cross-shaped bed that faces one shaped like the Star of David. A statue of Christ is in the center of the first bed, which is divided into twelve sections to represent the twelve disciples. Flora of the Old Testament grows around the statue of David, centered in the star-shaped plot. The twelve segments of this bed commemorate the tribes of Israel. From thirty to forty different biblical plants are represented in this garden of approximately twenty-five by fifty feet. Date palm, almond, fig, cypress, pomegranate, willow and apple trees grow here, as do cassia, mint, rosemary and other biblical herbs and spices.

Biblical Garden

San Antonio Botanical Gardens
555 Funston Pl.
San Antonio, TX 78209
Phone: 210-207-3250
Web site: www.sabot.org/bg
Open daily except Christmas Day and New Year's Day

Date palms, bay laurel and myrtle dot the landscape of plants mentioned in the Bible or cultivated in biblical times that grow in this compact garden, roughly thirty-eight by twenty-seven feet.

The DeWitt Memorial Fountain, centerpiece of the garden, is carved from volcanic stone. Vivid blues and burnt orange columns and pottery evoke a Mediterranean vista as visitors walk among the olive trees, oleanders and pomegranates or sit under cool grape arbors that cover the walkways. Miniature bulrushes, cypress grass, chicory and aloe thrive in shady areas. Marjoram, lavender and other sun-loving herbs are found in the adjoining Rose Garden. In the conservatory's Aquatic Garden, lotuses, water lilies and irises grow among other water-loving plants.

VERMONT

Biblical Gardens

First Congregational Church of Fair Haven
2 N. Park Pl.
Fair Haven, VT 05743
Phone: 802-265-8864 or 265-8605
Web site: www.sover.net/~hkfamily
Open daily May through October

A water garden is the centerpiece of this biblical garden, which stretches about 150 feet around the outside of the church. Papyri, tall reeds, rushes, irises and water lilies thrive here, as do the surrounding willows, date palms and fig trees. The bitter herbs, alliums and melons, hyssop, thistles, lentils and barley, olive and almond trees are among the Old Testament plants found in the larger garden. Daisies, anemones and lilies and other lilies of the field of the New Testament, the tithing herbs, mustard seed and grapevines also grow in the garden. Trees and garden benches surround the Children's Biblical Vegetable Garden, established in 1999 and laid out in a circular pattern.

VIRGINIA

Edward E. Kahn Memorial Biblical Garden
Temple Sinai
11620 Warwick Blvd.
Newport News, VA 23601
Phone: 757-596-8352
Web site: www.ujcvp.org/temple_sinai
Open daily

Begun in 1975 by Edward E. and Anna Lee Kahn after a trip to the Holy Land, this half-acre garden on the northwest side of the temple contains almost one hundred species of plant life that existed in the Holy Land more than two thousand years ago and are mentioned in the Bible.

Most of the plants are identified with plaques that give the Hebrew name, the common name, the botanical name and the verse in the Bible that refers to the plant. Oak, oleander, pine and olive trees grow here, as do styrax, tamarisk and many flowers, herbs and fragrant shrubs.

Canada

ALBERTA

Herb Garden, Devonian Botanic Garden

University of Alberta
Edmonton, Alberta T6G 2E1
Phone: 780-987-3054
Web site: www.devonian.ualberta.ca
Open daily May 1 through [Canadian] Thanksgiving weekend;
weekends only October 9 through December 2

First planted in 1977, the three-quarter-acre herb garden displays plants arranged by use in large island beds enclosed by a low, protective hedge of pygmy caragana. A number of biblical plants are found here. Flax is one of the economic plants, grown for manufacturing and industrial use. Wormwood, yellow flag, corn poppy and rue grow with other medicinal plants. Among the domestic herbs are rush, used for cleaning, flax for writing and worm-wood for animal care. Herbs used for cosmetic purposes include cucumber for eye care, flax for dry skin, marjoram for soap and nettle for hair care. Egyptian onion and chicory are in the edible group. Oregano, marjoram, cumin, sage and mints are used for cooking. Poisonous plants, including anemone, hemlock and opium poppy, are in a special bed.

ONTARIO

Biblical Garden
Temple Emanu-El

120 Old Colony Rd.
North York, Ontario M2L 2K2
Phone: 416-449-3880
Web site: http://feduja.org/commserv/organize/0222.stm
Call to arrange a visit

During morning service in the kiddush room, the congregation looks out on this serene and peaceful garden, created in an inner courtyard in 1972.

Water splashes in a small fountain, and bulrushes thrive in geometric pools. The mighty oak of Abraham, flowering almond, olive, pomegranate and fig trees, memorial peony and apricot trees bring biblical passages to life. Grapes harvested from the arbor are used at Sukkoth. Biblically named Jacob's ladder grows next to a large stone representing the rock where Jacob rested his head. Rue, laurel and oleander grow here, with local annuals interspersed for color.

Herb Garden
Niagara Parks Botanical Gardens
Niagara Pkwy.
Niagara Falls, Ontario L2E 6T2
Phone: 877-642-7275
Web site: www.niagaraparks.com
Open daily

Biblical plants are found throughout this one-acre hedged herb garden with twenty themed beds that include aromatic, culinary, poisonous and medicinal plants. Two small beds contain only Bible flora. Here are the bitter herbs and tithing herbs, alliums, coriander, ginger, lavender and wormwood. Aloe, oleander, opium poppy, thistle and other biblical herbs grow in other beds that surround a large sundial.

Mediterranean Garden
Royal Botanical Gardens
680 Plains Rd. West
Burlington/Hamilton, Ontario L7T 4H4
Phone: 905-527-1158
Web site: www.rbg.ca
Open daily; RBG Centre closed Christmas Day and New Year's Day

This two-level climate-controlled garden, located in the RBG Centre, is home to fig, olive, date palm, carob and pomegranate trees. Laurel, acacia, lilies and agapanthus are found in the upper level, while the lower level displays rue, myrtle, leeks, rosemary, thyme, oregano and other herbs and ground covers. Iris and papyrus are found here.

Many biblical herbs are in the medicinal garden in Hendrie Park, with groupings for cancer-fighting medicines and for the immune, gastrointestinal, nervous and respiratory systems. Flax, hyssop, coriander, sorrel, wormwood, garlic, poppy and rue grow here.

Medicinal Plant and Monastery Gardens
Montreal Botanical Garden
4101 Sherbrooke St. East
Montreal, Quebec H1X 2B2
Phone: 514-872-1400
Web site: www.ville.montreal.qc.ca/jardin
Open daily

The Medicinal Plant Garden includes one hundred plants used in folk medicine and provides information about the therapeutic properties of plants. Medicinal and aromatic plants from ancient times cultivated within the walls of cloisters in the Middle Ages are clustered around the central well in the Monastery Garden. Biblical plants include wild ginger and spearmint. Culinary plants from the Mediterranean and other parts of the world are found in the Economic Plants Garden. The Montreal Botanical Garden was created in 1931.

Israel

Neot Kedumim
PO Box 1007
Lod, Israel 71110
Phone: 972-8-977-0777
Web site: www.neot-kedumim.org.il
Closed Saturdays and Israel State holidays

Natural and agricultural landscapes recreate the physical setting of the Bible in the 625-acre Biblical Landscape Reserve located ten minutes from Ben Gurion Airport, near Modi'in on Route 443. In 1971 Israeli botanist Nogah Hareuveni began the work of transforming mostly barren rock into a network of pastoral landscapes representing regions of ancient Israel and themes of the Bible. Visitors can choose from three self-guided tours of approximately two hours each and there is a handicapped-accessible trail. Trail guide booklets give biblical, historical and botanical information. A trail map includes a partial listing of 125 plants found in the reserve.

Trail A winds past village excavations and the village olive press, a family winepress and vineyard and the Pool of Solomon. An ancient olive tree, fig trees, a caper bush, carob, myrtle, white broom, Sharon tulip and narcissus can be seen along the way. Cedars of Lebanon grow alongside clumps of hyssop in the Garden of Wisdom Literature.

Trail B stops at an olive press with a crushing wheel and basin dating to Roman times and a winepress that may belong to a Jewish settlement of the Second Temple period currently being excavated. Moriah or living menorah (sage) plants grow above and below the Hill of the Menorah. Plants producing fragrant spices are found in an area called the Ascent of Spices. A pomegranate grove, a patch of mandrakes, almond trees and an olive grove can be seen along the trail. Olive trees grow on terraced hillsides.

Trail C re-creates the "land of milk and honey" with the seven varieties (wheat, barley, grapevines, fig trees, pomegranates, olive trees, date honey) mentioned in Moses' description of the Promised Land. Along the trail are a Sukkoth booth and the four species it requires, a grove of date palm trees and the Pool of the Willows, surrounded by willow, Euphrates poplar and mountain poplar trees.

Terraced hillside with olive trees,
Neot Kedumim, Lod, Israel

The World of the Bible Gardens

13 Ahayot St.
PO Box 2329
Jerusalem, Israel 91022
Phone: 972-2-643-0196.
Web site: www.brusa.org
Open daily

Full-scale archaeological replicas of a sheepfold, watchtower, grape press, threshing floor, well and cistern and other biblical reference points in the Bible Gardens help visitors interpret the Scriptures. The gardens include papyrus and bulrush-filled pools and waterfalls, grape arbors and a five-hundred-year-old olive tree. Among other Bible plants found here are almond, fig and pomegranate trees.

Biblical Garden

St. George's College, Jerusalem
31 Salahedeen St.
Jerusalem, Israel 91190
Phone: 972-2-626-4704
E-mail: college@stgeorges.org.il
Open daily

Established in 1990, this garden covers approximately twenty-five hundred square meters. F. Nigel Hepper, research botanist at Kew Herbarium in England, planned the garden, which is laid out in four sections and includes a tamarisk garden, olive garden with trees from Roman times, fruit garden with figs and pomegranates, a myrtle garden and cedars of Lebanon garden. Grapevines cover an arbor. Oleander, wormwood and white broom also grow here. The garden is a short walk from the Damascus Gate.

Great Britain

ENGLAND

Bible Garden
St. Michael's Convent
56 Ham Common, Richmond, Surrey TW10 7JH
Phone: 02089 408711
E-mail: robin.csc@themutual.net
Web site: www.tap.net/csc
Open Quiet Garden days:
First Tuesday of each month May to October; call for other days.

Inspired and envisioned in 1988 by Sister Margaret Richelois, c.s.c., the garden was created over the following two years to represent "The Seven Circles of Prayer." Biblical plants include lilies of the field and other flowers: anemones, lilies, poppies and roses; bitter herbs; garlic, leeks and onions; grapevine; palm, fig, bay, pomegranate and olive trees; juniper, lavender, myrtle, rue sage and wormwood. Plants are labeled and a handbook provides the biblical references and lore for each plant. The garden is now double the original size.

Quiet Garden
Aston Tirrold Centre for Reflection
Spring Lane, Aston Tirrold, Didcot, Oxfordshire OX11 9EJ
Phone: 01235 850423
Web site: www.reflect.freeuk.com
Open every third Thursday of the month from 10 a.m.–4 p.m.
Call for other days.

Water runs down one side of a rock into a small pool filled with large cobbles and surrounded by stones, evoking images of healing in the Pool of Siloam, waters of baptism and Moses striking the rock. Bulrushes, linked to Moses, grow at poolside in this garden. Biblical plants are among the Mediterranean type flora and more are being identified and added to the garden, designed in 1998.

Quiet Garden

Bulwick Rectory
Corby, Northamptonshire NN17 3DY
Phone: 01780 450249
Open under the National Garden Scheme; private appointments available

The garden, which covers an area of about two acres, including house and paddock, has evolved over the last twenty-three years. A Journey of Life garden, begun in 1999, makes use of existing features. A dovecote represents the Cave of Birth, the folly denotes the summit of Early Bliss, a pond reflects the heavens, and trees embody the Tree of Learning. Old Testament plants in the garden include rose of Sharon, lily of the valley, and apple, cypress, oak, pine, mulberry, fig and nut trees. Mustard seed, coriander, wheat, fig and vine, all used in parables, are some of the plants of the Gospels found in the garden. Some plants included are: adam-and-eve *(Pulmonaria officinalis),* Adam's needle *(Yucca filementosa),* Jacob's ladder *(Polemonium),* Jerusalem sage *(Phlomis fruticosa),* Jerusalem cross *(Lychnis chalcedoniac)* and Solomon's seal *(Polgyonatum).*

Quiet Garden

Stoke Park Farm
Park Road, Stoke Poges, Buckinghamshire SL2 4PG
Phone: 01753 643050
Web site: www.quietgarden.co.uk
E-mail: quietgarden@ukonline.co.uk
Open Thursdays during term time
(not during summer, Christmas and Easter holidays)

At Stoke Poges, the headquarters of the Quiet Garden Trust, the hostess has installed a number of plants and labeled them with a plaque and a quotation from Scripture. The garden is very informal and contains lily, poppy, rockrose, hyssop, saffron and mint as well as myrtle, grape vines, white broom and brambles. Biblical trees in the garden include almond, fig, oak, pine, olive, walnut and the Judas tree.

Temperate House, Aquatic Garden, Juniper Collection, Royal Botanic Gardens

Kew, Richmond, Surrey TW9 3AB
Phone: 02083 325000
Web site: www.rbgkew.org.uk
Open daily except Christmas Day and New Year's Day

Many of the gardens and collections at Kew, comprising 120 hectares (300 acres), contain biblical plants. The south wing of the Temperate House displays Mediterranean and African plants, and the center holds many tall subtropical trees and palms. Forty different varieties of water lily are in the main tank of the Aquatic Garden, and sedges and rushes are found in corner tanks. More water lilies are in the Waterlily House. A representative collection of sixty species and cultivars of juniper are in seven beds of the Juniper Collection. Quince, apple, pear and willow trees and rockroses grow in the Secluded Garden, and quince and anemone are found in the Winter Garden.

SCOTLAND

The Biblical Garden

Cooper Park (adjacent to Elgin Cathedral)
King St.
Elgin, Moray
Phone: 01343 563367; 01343 543451
Open daily May through September

Designed in the shape of a Celtic cross, this three-acre garden, the first of its kind in Scotland, was established in 1996. All 110 plants mentioned in the Bible are found here. Distinct areas of the garden highlight the mountains, fertile valleys, deserts and marshland of the Holy Land. Mount Sinai and the cave of the resurrection are depicted. Life-size sculptures portray the parables of the Sower, the Prodigal Son, the woman at the well, Samson and the Good Shepherd. A basket symbolizing the saving of the infant Moses is found among the rushes in a tiny pool. Poppies, cornflowers and daisies representing the lilies of the field grow in raised beds along the west wall and vegetables of the Bible are in beds behind the main floral displays. Biblical trees and shrubs are placed along south and east walls.

Bible Plants in Your Garden

If you have a garden, some biblical plants may already be growing there. Tithing herbs and bitter herbs may be there. Lilies of the field and valley may bloom there.

What grows in your garden is determined by climate and to some degree by the terrain and soil. Some biblical plants grew in marshes, others in tropical deserts. Growing conditions differ in the eastern and western parts of the United States and Canada as well as in the north and south. What thrives in Arizona, California or Texas may not grow in England or Scotland.

Several botanists and gardening experts have written books specifically about planting Bible flora and Bible gardens. F. Nigel Hepper, Eleanor Anthony King and Allan A. Swenson suggest species to look for, how and where to plant and how to adjust for climate. Their books are found listed in the bibliography. In addition to regional books, such as the Sunset Western Garden Book, *comprehensive volumes such as the* Reader's Digest New Illustrated Guide to Gardening in Canada *and the* U.S. National Arboretum's Book of Outstanding Garden Plants, *recommend plants and varieties for every region and growing zone of their countries.*

Appendix: More Healing Plants

Acacia nilotica
Acacia, Egyptian mimosa

"There the angel of the Lord appeared to him in a flame of fire out of a bush..."
—Exodus 3:2

The Hebrew word for bush is *seneh* or *sneh*, meaning "a prickly bush." The burning bush described is thought to be the thorny acacia or Egyptian mimosa covered with the acacia strap-flower, a crimson-flowered mistletoe that grows on various thorny acacia shrubs and trees in the Holy Land. Useful in treatment of diabetes.

Prunus dulcis
Almond

"...the staff of Aaron for the house of Levi had sprouted.
It put forth buds, produced blossoms, and bore ripe almonds."
—Numbers 17:8

Flowering and thriving almond trees symbolize the growth and endurance of the Jews and bitter almonds remind them of the days of slavery. The oil is used for flavoring baked goods, candies and medicine. Used in the treatment of cancer.

Prunus armeniaca
Apricot, Chinese almond

"A word fitly spoken is like apples of gold in pictures of silver...."
—Proverbs 25:11

Some scholars believe the apricot is the biblical apple because it is fragrant, sweet, has a golden color and is so abundant in the Holy Land. The Hebrew word used is *tappuach*. Used in treatment of cancer.

Laurus nobilis
Bay leaf, sweet bay, Grecian laurel

"I have seen the wicked oppressing, and towering like a cedar of Lebanon."
—Psalm 37:35

Some versions of the Bible translate *ezrach*, meaning "a native shrub," as "cedar of Lebanon," which is *erez* in Hebrew, but biblical scholars believe it is the sweet-bay or laurel tree and translate the phrase as "spreading himself like a green bay tree." Bay leaves are used for flavoring meats and stews. Used in treatment of diabetes.

Citrullus colocynthis
Bitter apple, colocynth, gall, wild gourd

"They offered him wine to drink, mixed with gall."
—Matthew 27:34

The fruit of this trailing vine, which grows wild in the desert, is intensely bitter and poisonous and was thought to be offered to Jesus because of its bitter taste. It is used medicinally as a cathartic and for constipation.

Brassica nigra
Black mustard

"The kingdom of God...is like a mustard seed that someone took and sowed in the garden; it grew and became a tree, and the birds of the air made nests in its branches."
—Luke 13:18–19

Where there is no frost, this annual shrub can grow to tree-like proportions in the Holy Land, with thick stems and branches to shelter birds. Eighteenth-century travelers reported the plant was as high as a horse and his rider, and birds rested on it. The parable illustrates the increase of Christ's kingdom from small beginnings. It is used to treat bronchitis, colds and cancer.

Cyperus papyrus
Bulrush, papyrus

"When she could hide him no longer she got a papyrus basket for him,
and plastered it with bitumen and pitch; she put the child in it
and placed it among the reeds on the bank of the river."
—Exodus 2:3

Papyrus stems were used for making light boats and were the main source of material for making paper in ancient Greece. The name *paper* derives from the word *papyrus*. It is used in folk medicine for inflammation of the eyes, for cancer and sores.

Vetiveria zizanioides
Calamus, sweet cane

"Of what use to me is frankincense that comes from Sheba,
or sweet cane from a distant land?"
—Jeremiah 6:20

The Hebrew words *kaneh-bosem* and *kaneh-hattob*, meaning "reed of fragrance" and "fragrant reed," are translated "sweet cane." The word *kaneh* is similar to the Latin *canna*, and the Greek *calamos*. The plant, a native of India, was an ingredient of the anointing oil used in the temple. In folk medicine it was used for boils, burns, colic, fever and flu.

Capparis spinosa
Caper

"When one is afraid of heights, and terrors are in the road;
the almond tree blossoms, the grasshopper drags itself along and desire fails."
—Ecclesiastes 12:5

The flower buds of the caper bush were called "desire shall fail" because eating them weakened the appetite and staved off hunger until the main course arrived. The biblical verse refers to old age, when even capers fail to excite the appetite. Pickled capers are used as a spice. The juice of the plant is said to be effective against bacteria and fungus.

Ceratonia siliqua

Carob

"Now John wore clothing of camel's hair with a leather belt around his waist, and his food was locusts and wild honey."

—John 3:4

Pods of carob seeds were called "St. John's Bread"—"locusts" in the Bible. They were primarily used as animal feed, but humans ate them during times of famine. When ripe they are full of a sweet, honey-like syrup. The "husks" eaten by the Prodigal Son were empty carob pods. Carob seeds help inflammations of the throat and head and are used against cancer.

Cedrus libani

Cedar of Lebanon

"Consider Assyria, a cedar of Lebanon, with fair branches and forest shade, and of great heights, its top among the clouds."

—Ezekiel 31:3

In various passages of the Old Testament (2 Samuel, 1 Kings, 1 and 2 Chronicles) we read of the cedars of Lebanon sent by Hiram, King of Tyre, for the building of David's house, of the temple at Jerusalem, and of Solomon's house. A wide-spreading evergreen tree, the cedar grows one hundred feet or more in height. Cedars are mentioned seventy times in the Bible, were called "trees of the Lord" and were used to demonstrate God's power. In folk medicine cedar is used for asthma, bronchitis, burns and dermatitis.

Etrog, Citrus medica

Citron

"On the first day you shall take the fruit of majestic trees, branches of palm trees, boughs of leafy trees, and willows of the brook."

—Leviticus 23:40

Citron is considered one of the fruits of "majestic trees," translated "goodly trees" in other versions of the Bible. It is used in ceremonies associated with the Feast of the Tabernacles and is one of the traditional symbols of Judaism, its many seeds representing fertility. The sweet-smelling *Etrog* symbolizes Jews who are credited with both learning and good deeds. Used as a folk remedy for indigestion, lumbago and seasickness.

Coriandrum sativum
Coriander

"The house of Israel called it manna; it was like coriander seed, white, and the taste of it was like wafers made with honey."
—*Exodus 16:31*

Coriander grows wild in the Holy Land. It is an annual with small round grayish-colored seeds with white flowers so perhaps the manna was white like coriander flowers. The aromatic seeds are used as a spice in cooking and for indigestion in medicine.

Chrysanthemum coronarium
Crown Daisy

"For the sun rises with its scorching heat and withers the field;
its flower falls, and its beauty perishes.
It is the same way with the rich;
in the midst of a busy life, they will wither away."
—*James 1:10*

James, like Jesus, compares the transient flowers of the field to the short life of man, especially the proud. The yellow crown daisy still grows in the fields and along roadsides, drying up and withering away with the heat. Used in treatment of AIDS, melanoma and indigestion.

Paliuris spina-christi
Crown of Thorns

"So Jesus came out, wearing the crown of thorns and the purple robe."
—*John 19:5*

This scraggly shrub has flexible branches and sharp, irregular spines. The exceptionally pliable young branches of this plant make it easy to weave into a crown-like wreath. The plant was used as an astringent, diuretic and a tonic. In Christian tradition the Christ-thorn (*Ziziphys spina-christi*) is the "crown of thorns" mentioned in the Gospels.

Cucumis sativus
Cucumber

*"And daughter Zion is left like a booth in a vineyard,
like a shelter in a cucumber field, like a besieged city."*
—Isaiah 1:8

The Hebrews longed for the cucumbers of Egypt. The refreshing vegetable was so important in biblical times as a vegetable that cucumber fields were protected by guard posts to keep out thieves and wild animals. Cucumbers were one of the staples of food in Egypt and later in the Holy Land, especially among the poor. Cucumber slices relieve eye irritations, rashes and sunburn.

Cupressus sempervirens
Cypress

"Make yourself an ark of cypress wood; make rooms in the ark..."
—Genesis 6:9

The cypress tree was valuable for its durable wood. Cypress was sent by King Hiram to Solomon for building the temple of Jerusalem. The cypress doors of St. Peter's in Rome, more than twelve-hundred years old, show no signs of decay. Used in folk medicine for bronchitis, indigestion and hemorrhoids.

Matricaria aurea
Dog Chamomile

*"The grass withers,
and the flower falls,
but the word of the Lord endures forever."*
—1 Peter 1:24

This low-growing annual, with tiny yellow blossoms, is thought to have been one of the flowers of the fields, growing among the wheat and other grains, withering with the heat. Like German chamomile, it is used in folk medicine for a variety of ailments, from cold to fever and headache, to toothache and wounds.

Linum usitatissimum
Flax

"David danced before the Lord with all his might;
David was girded with a linen ephod."
—2 Samuel 6:14

Flax, the oldest textile fiber known to man, was the main textile fabric used in biblical times. Jewish women made linen from the fibers and wove them into the robes and aprons worn by the priests and temple attendants. The fibers were also used as wicks for lamps and mummy wrappings. The word linen comes from the Latin or Greek root meaning flax. The plant grows to four feet and bears small, deep or pale blue flowers. Flax seeds are used in poultices for abscesses, burns and rheumatism. The oil prevents inflammation and tumor growths and boosts the immune system.

Boswellia carteri, B. papyrifera
Frankincense, Olibanum

"...with all trees of frankincense, myrrh and aloes...."
—Song of Solomon 4:13

Frankincense, an important ingredient in the incense used in the temple, was imported by the Hebrews via the spice route that crossed southern Arabia. It was one of the gifts of the wise men to the infant Jesus, symbolizing his holiness and divinity, and is now used as incense in ceremonies of the Catholic church. In folk medicine it is used as a diuretic and for stomachaches, bronchitis and rheumatism.

Cymbopogon martini
Ginger Grass, Aromatic Cane

"The LORD spoke to Moses: take the finest spices...
and two hundred fifty of aromatic cane.
...make of these a sacred anointing oils...."
—Exodus 3:22–25

Aromatic grasses were used for the sacred anointing oil, in perfumes and cosmetics, and for flavoring. Ginger grass, native to India, would have been one of the products brought from "a far country" (Jeremiah 6:20). Ginger grass oil was used medicinally in ancient times.

Lawsonia inermis
Henna, Camphire

"My beloved is to me a cluster of henna blossoms
in the vineyards of En-gedi."
—Song of Solomon 1:14

One of the earliest known spices and perfumes, henna grew in King Solomon's garden. The dried leaves produce a red dye, first used by the Egyptians as a cosmetic. Bunches of small, fragrant, white flowers appear in the spring on this tree-like shrub, which has disappeared from En-Gedi but is still found in Jericho, the Jordan Valley and on the coastal plain. The leaves are used to treat sore throats, diarrhea and to prevent hemorrhaging. Henna plasters help bacterial and fungal infections.

Hedera helix
Ivy

"The Jews...were compelled to wear wreaths of ivy
and to walk in the procession in honor of Dionysus."
—2 Maccabees 6:7

Ivy has long been associated with religious rites and festivals. The ancient Greeks dedicated it to Bacchus and sprigs of ivy symbolized friendship. The climbing shrub is now rare in Israel, found only in Upper Galilee and Samaria. Christians began to use it at Christmastime and the evergreen vine became a symbol of everlasting life. Used in folk medicine for corns, malaria, rheumatism and toothache.

Anastatica hierochuntica
Jericho Rose, Mary's Flower, Palestinian Tumbleweed

"O my God, make them like whirling dust (or a tumbleweed),
like chaff before the wind."
—Psalm 83:13

The Hebrew word *gulgal*, sometimes translated as "dust" or "a wheel," refers to a plant, probably the Palestinian tumbleweed, which grows abundantly around Jericho and the Mediterranean region. After blooming the plant dries up and forms a hollow ball that is blown about by the wind until it reaches moisture and sprouts again. In folk medicine it is used for colds and epilepsy.

Cynomorium coccineum
Juniper

"They pick mallow and the leaves of bushes,
and to warm themselves the roots of broom."
—Job 30:4

The Hebrew words are *r'tamim sho'resh,* "roots of the broom-bush." Some biblical versions translate this as juniper, a species of broom that is quite nauseous and somewhat poisonous. Scholars speculate that the people might have gathered what they thought were juniper roots but was really *Cynomorium coccineum,* a parasitic plant which grows in salt marshes and maritime sands. In ancient days it was valued for the treatment of dysentery. In folk medicine it is used for colic, constipation, sterility and dysentery.

Tamarix aphylla
Leafless Tamarisk

"Abraham planted a tamarisk tree in Beersheba,
and called there on the name of the Lord, the Everlasting God."
—Genesis 21:33

Beersheba, where Abraham planted the tamarisk, is known for its droughts. The richly-branched evergreen tamarisk, partial to dry and sandy environments, is grown for its shade throughout the Negev but is also valued for its wood. It is indigenous in the wadies of the Araveh Valley. The astringent, bitter bark is mixed with oil and used to treat eczema, scratched eyes and other conditions.

Lactuca sativa
Lettuce

"Eat it with unleavened bread and bitter herbs."
—Numbers 9:11

Leaves of garden lettuce can be bitter when left too long in the ground and some sources cite lettuce as one of the bitter herbs of Passover. The children of Israel probably adopted the custom of eating bitter herbs with their meat and bread from the Egyptians, who dipped bread into a mixture of green herbs and mustard. Used in the treatment of insomnia, coughs and cancer.

Atriplex halimus
Mallow, Sea Purslane

"They pick mallow and the leaves of bushes...."
—Job 30:4

The Hebrew word *malluach*, implying salted, is translated as "mallows." Sea purslane or shrubby orach is a bushy shrub related to spinach that grows on the shores of the Mediterranean and around the Dead Sea. Hungry shepherds were said to eat it. The Talmud indicates that mallows were a staple in the diet of men working on the reconstruction of the Temple in the first century B.C. It is used medicinally for sores and ulcers, gastric acidity and dermatitis.

Mandragora officinarum
Mandrake

"The mandrakes give forth fragrance...."
—Song of Solomon 7:13

The mandrake plant, slightly poisonous, was considered a symbol of fertility in biblical times. The yellow fruit, called a love apple, has a peculiar smell and sickeningly sweet taste. Because the roots resemble a human torso, the plant has been the source of much superstition. The Jews considered it a charm against evil spirits. The leaves were said to shine in the dark, and the Arabs still call the plant "devil's candles." The plant is both sedative and aphrodisiac in effect, was used as an anesthetic and has been used to treat tumors, ulcers and rheumatism.

Cucumis melo
Muskmelon

"We remember the fish we used to eat in Egypt...the cucumbers, the melons..."
—Numbers 11:5

The Hebrew *kishuim* and *mikshah* are said to refer not to cucumbers but to muskmelons, originally cultivated in East Africa. The juicy fruit is highly prized in hot dry climates where it is eaten directly from the rind or sprinkled with sugar or ginger as a dessert. All parts of the plant are used medicinally: the fruit for eczema, the rind for stomach tumors and cancer, the root for cancers, the flowers to cause vomiting and the stalks to relieve it.

Myrtus communis
Myrtle

"I will put in the wilderness the cedar, the acacia, the myrtle, and the olive...."
—Isaiah 41:19

The Hebrew word for myrtle is *hadas*, meaning "sweetness." It is one of the four species gathered for the Feast of Tabernacles. A symbol of peace, immortality and divine generosity, myrtle was popular in biblical names and its name was given to both men (*assa*) and women (*hadassah*). The evergreen shrub is valued for its fragrant flowers, leaves and bark, used in perfumes, cooking and medicine. Tincture of myrtle is used to cleanse incisions and relieve swollen joints. Used to treat tuberculosis, smallpox, asthma and cancer.

Narcissus tazetta
Narcissus, Biblical Rose

"I am a rose of Sharon, a lily of the valleys."
—Song of Solomon 2:1

Many scholars believe that the "rose of Sharon" was the narcissus, which grows abundantly on the plain of Sharon. The Hebrew word *chabazzeleth*, meaning "bulb," has been erroneously translated as "rose" in many versions of the Bible. The "rose" of Ecclesiastes was a spring-flowering bulb, not a true rose. In pictures of the Annunciation, the narcissus sometimes replaces the lily. Plant extracts are used for perfume, skin lotion and to treat cancer and fever.

Nerium oleander
Oleander, Biblical Rose

*"Listen to me, my faithful children,
and blossom like a rose growing by a stream of water."*
—Sirach 39:13

Found in great abundance around the lakes of Galilee and Tiberius and along the Jordan River, the oleander is considered to be the "rose growing by a stream." The blossoms look like roses from a distance. The oleander is the floral symbol for Saint Joseph. In folk medicine it treats dermatitis, edema, hypertension and ringworm.

Elaeagnus angustifolia

Oleaster, Russian Olive

"Will the Lord be pleased with thousands of rams,
with ten thousands of rivers of oil?"
—Micah 6:7

The oil referred to in Micah is thought to be a product of the oleaster, which yields an oil used as a medication rather than a food. The Hebrew word used is *etz shamen,* translated as "oil tree" or "olive tree," while *zayit* is used for the true olive. It is sometimes called wild olive but has no relationship to the true olive. The fruit is either small and tasteless or olive-sized and bitter. The oil is used for burns, constipation, fever and wounds.

Rosa Phonecia

Phoenician Rose

"I grew tall like a palm tree in Engedi, and like rosebushes in Jericho."
—Sirach 24:14

This plant, which grows on riverbanks and along brooks in the Mediterranean, was grown in gardens during biblical times. It is one of four species of rose native to Israel. The Talmud speaks of "rose gardens that have existed there since the Early Prophets." The rose hips and petals of this species are rich in vitamins and are used to treat scurvy.

Arundo donax

Reed, Persian Reed, Spanish Cane

"What did you go out into the wilderness to look at? A reed shaken by the wind?"
—Matthew 11:7

The giant reed is a gigantic grass, growing from eight to eighteen feet, with a beautiful plume of white flowers. Authorities believe that the words *agmon, agam* and *agamim,* used to represent most of the reeds of the Bible, refer to this species. It grows near water and the stems are used to make trellises and supports for vines and climbing plants. In folk medicine it is used for cancer, dropsy and hypertension.

Ficus sycomorus

Sycamore, Egyptian Sycamore, Mulberry Fig

"He was trying to see who Jesus was,
but on account of the crowd he could not,
because he was short in stature.
So he ran ahead and climbed a sycamore tree to see him..."
—Luke 19:3–4

The tree that Zacchaeus climbed has fruit like the true fig and leaves like the mulberry tree. The name comes from *sycon*, fig, and *moron*, mulberry. The fruit is inferior to the fig, but the porous, lightweight and durable wood was used for temples and coffins. The lofty tree is reported to have opened to receive and protect the Virgin Mary and her son Jesus from pursuing soldiers. Latex from the tree was used for burns, cancers and tumors.

Astragallus gummifer, A. tragacantha

Tragacanth, Gum

"Then they sat down to eat; and looking up they saw
a caravan of Ishmaelites coming from Gilead,
with their camels carrying gum, balm, and resin,
on their way to carry it down to Egypt."
—Genesis 37:25

Tragacanth is translated as either "spice" or "gum" in the Bible, and the *nekhoth* that was carried with other spices from Gilead was probably a product of tragacanth. The gum, exuded from the root of the spiny shrub and dried, is used in toothpaste, hand lotions, syrups, salad dressings and sauces. It is a remedy for burns, coughs and diarrhea and is thought to strongly inhibit cancer cells.

Citrullus lanatus

Watermelon

"We remember the fish we used to eat in Egypt...the cucumbers, the melons..."
—Numbers 11:5

Some say that the Hebrew *avatihim* should be translated as "watermelons," not "melons," the meaning still given it by Arab villagers. The Egyptians and Israelites grew watermelons in ancient times, using them as food, drink and medicine. The juice made a refreshing beverage and the fruit, relished by rich and poor, was also used as a laxative. Oil from the seeds was used in salads, cooking and in lamps. Roasted and salted seeds are still a popular side dish. In folk medicine watermelon treated fever, cystitis and indigestion.

Artemisia herba-alba
White wormwood

"The thought of my affliction and my homelessness is wormwood and gall!"
—*Lamentations 3:19*

Even though wormwood and gall are mentioned as separate substances in Scripture, some believe wormwood is the bitter gall mentioned in Matthew 27:34. Because wormwood has a bitter taste, it became a symbol of bitter calamity and sorrow for the Hebrews. This species is common in Palestine today, and is used against intestinal worms, as its name suggests. The Egyptians use it for tapeworms and camels that graze on wormwood are said to resist skin diseases.

Bibliography

Addison, Josephine. *The Illustrated Plant Lore.* London: Sidgwick and Jackson, 1985.

Allen, H. C. *Key Notes.* New Delhi, India: B. Jain Publishers, 1989.

Alon, Azaria. *Flowers and Trees of the Holy Land.* Israel: Palphot, n.d.

Anderson, A. W. *Plants of the Bible.* London: Crosby Lockwood and Son, 1956.

Arano, Luisa. *The Medieval Health Handbook.* New York: George Braziller, 1996.

Balfour, John Hutton. *The Plants of the Bible.* London: T. Nelson and Sons, 1866.

Ball, Ann. *Catholic Traditions in the Garden.* Huntington, Ind.: Our Sunday Visitor, 1998.

Bar-Adon, Pessah. *The Cave of the Treasure: The Finds from the Caves in Nahal Mishmar.* Jerusalem: Israel Exploration Society, 1980.

Berrall, Julia S. *The Garden.* New York: Viking Press, 1966.

Boland, Maureen and Bridget Boland. *Old Wives' Lore for Gardeners.* New York: Farrar, Strauss and Giroux, 1976.

Brewer, Sunshine. *Mother Nature's Emporium.* Ohio: privately printed, 1989.

Bromiley, Geoffrey W. ed. *International Standard Bible Encyclopedia.* Grand Rapids, Mich.: W. B. Eerdmans, 1979.

Callcott, Maria. *Scripture Herbal.* London: Longman, Brown, Green, and Longmans, 1842.

Cerruti. *The Four Seasons of the House of Cerruti.* New York: Facts on File Publications, 1984.

Chancellor, John. *The Flowers and Fruits of the Bible.* New York: Beaufort Books, 1982.

Chevallier, Andrew. *Encyclopedia of Medicinal Plants.* New York: DK Publishing, 1996.

Coats, Alice M. *Flowers and Their Histories.* New York: McGraw-Hill Book Co., 1956.

Coats, Peter. *Flowers in History.* New York: Viking Press, 1970.

Conway, David. *The Magic of Herbs.* New York: E. P. Dutton and Co., 1973.

Coon, Nelson. *Using Plants for Healing.* New York: Hearthside Press, 1963.

Crowfoot, Grace M. and Louise Baldensperger. *From Cedar to Hyssop: A Study in the Folklore of Plants in Palestine.* London: Sheldon Press, 1932.

D'Andrea, Jeanne. *Ancient Herbs in the J. Paul Getty Museum Gardens.* Malibu, Calif.: J. Paul Getty Museum, 1989.

Danin, Avinoum, and Gideon Orshan. *Vegetation of Israel.* Leiden, Netherlands: Backhuup Publications, 1999.

Darom, David. *Beautiful Plants of the Bible.* Herzlia, Israel: Palphot, n.d.

Davies, Gill and John Cule. *Timetables of Medicine.* New York: Black Dog and Leventhal, 2000.

Davies, W. Vivian and Roxie Walker, eds. *Biological Anthropology and the Study of Ancient Egypt.* London: British Museum Press, 1993.

Davis, Avram, and Manuela Dunn Mascetti. *Judaic Mysticism.* New York: Hyperion, 1997.

Dejey, M. A. *Health Plants of the World: Atlas of Medicinal Plants.* New York: Newsweek Books, 1979.

de Waal, Marinus, *Medicinal Herbs in the Bible.* York Beach, Maine: Samuel Weiser, 1984.

Duke, James. *Biblical Botany.* [Online] *Available at* http://www.ars-grin.gov/duke/syllabus/module12.

____. *Herbs of the Bible.* Loveland, Colo: Interweave Press, 1999.

____. *Medicinal Plants of the Bible.* New York: Trado-Medic Books, 1983.

Eliade, Mircea, ed. *Encyclopedia of Religion.* New York: MacMillan Publishing, 1987.

Emboden, William A., Jr. *Art and Artifact as Ethnobotanical Tools in the Ancient Near East with Emphasis on Psychoactive Plants.* [Online] *Available at* http://www.gnosticgarden.com/articles/art.

Farb, Peter. *The Land, Wildlife, and Peoples of the Bible.* New York: Harper and Row, 1967.

Fleming, Jim. *The World of the Bible Gardens.* Jerusalem, Israel: Biblical Resources, 1999.

Foggi, Bruno. *Flowers of Israel.* Florence, Italy: Casa Editrice Bonechi, 1999.

Foster, Steven, and James Duke. *Eastern/Central Medicinal Plants.* Boston: Houghton Mifflin, 1990.

Freedman, David Noel, ed. *The Anchor Bible Dictionary.* New York: Doubleday, 1992.

Freeman, James M. *Manners and Customs of the Bible.* Plainfield, N. J.: Logos International, 1972.

Frenkley, Helen. "The Search for Roots." *Biblical Archaeology Review.* September / October 1986.

____. *Self-Guided Tour, Trail A.* Lod, Israel: Neot Kedumim, 1999.

_____. *Self-Guided Tour, Trail B*. Lod, Israel: Neot Kedumim, 1996.

_____. *Self-Guided Tour, Trail C*. Lod, Israel: Neot Kedumim, 1996.

Gaer, Joseph. *Lore of the New Testament*. Boston: Little, Brown and Co., 1952.

_____. *Lore of the Old Testament*. New York: Grossett and Dunlap, 1951.

Gerard, John. *Herbal*. London: Studio Editions, 1994.

Gilmer, Maureen. *Rooted in the Spirit*. Dallas: Taylor Publishing, 1997.

Ginzberg, Louis. *Legends of the Bible*. Philadelphia: Jewish Publication Society of America, 1956.

Goodman, Naomi, Robert Marcus, and Susan Woolhandler, *The Good Book Cookbook*. Grand Rapids, Mich.: Baker Book House, 1995.

Gordon, Lesley. *A Country Herbal*. New York: Mayflower Books, 1980.

_____. *Green Magic*. New York: Viking Press, 1977.

Greenblatt, Robert B. *Search the Scriptures*. Philadelphia: J. B. Lippincott, 1977.

Hareuveni, Nogah. *Ecology in the Bible*. Kiryat Ono, Israel: Neot Kedumim, 1988.

_____. *Desert and Shepherd in Our Biblical Heritage*. Kiryat Ono, Israel: Neot Kedumim, 1991.

_____. *Nature in Our Biblical Heritage*. Kiryat Ono, Israel: Neot Kedumim, 1996.

_____. *Tree and Shrub in Our Biblical Heritage*. Kiryat Ono, Israel: Neot Kedumim, 1989.

Harris, Thaddeus Mason. *The Natural History of the Bible*. London: privately printed, 1824.

Harrison, R. H., *Healing Herbs of the Bible*. Leiden, Netherlands: E. J. Brill, 1966.

Hasnas, Rachelle. *The Essence of Bach Flowers*. Freedom, Calif.: Crossing Press, 1999.

Hepper, F. Nigel. *Baker Encyclopedia of Bible Plants*. Grand Rapids, Mich.: Baker Book House, 1992.

_____. *Bible Plants at Kew*. London: Her Majesty's Stationery Office, 1985.

_____. *Lands of the Bible*. Nashville: Thomas Nelson Publishers, 1995.

_____. *Planting a Bible Garden*. London: Her Majesty's Stationery Office, 1987.

Hettinger, Mary Ellen. *Home Remedies from the Bible*. Boca Raton, Fla.: Globe Communications, 1995.

Hutchens, Alma R. *Indian Herbalogy of North America*. Boston: Shambhala, 1991.

Jacob, Irene. *Botanical Symbols in World Religions*. Pittsburgh, Penn.: Rodef Shalom Press, 2001.

Jacob, Walter, and Irene Jacob, eds. *The Healing Past: Pharmaceuticals in the Biblical and Rabbinic World*. New York: E. J. Brill, 1993.

James, Wilma. *Gardening with Biblical Plants*. Chicago: Nelson-Hall, 1983.

Kains, M. G. *Culinary Herbs, Their Cultivation, Harvesting, Curing and Uses*. London: Kegan Paul, Trench, Trubner and Co., 1912.

Kavasch, E. Barrie and Karen Baar. *American Indian Healing Arts*. New York: Bantam Books, 1999.

Keller, Werner. *The Bible as History*. New York: William Morrow and Co., 1981.

King, Eleanor Anthony. *Bible Plants for American Gardens*. New York: Dover Publications, 1975.

Koepke, Ann. *Herbs and Flowers in the Bible*. Cincinnati: Forward Movement Publications, 1990.

Lamsa, George M. *New Testament Light*. San Francisco: Harper and Row, 1988.

Larkey, Sanford, and Thomas Pyles. *An Herbal (1525)*. New York: Scholars' Facsimiles and Reprints, 1941.

Liberty Hyde Bailey Hortorium, Cornell University. *Hortus Third: A Concise Dictionary of Plants Cultivated in the United States and Canada*. New York: Macmillan Publishing, 1976.

Lust, Benedict. *Kniepp Herbs and Their Uses*. Beaumont, Calif.: Benedict Lust Publications, 1968.

MacKay, Alistair. *Farming and Gardening in the Bible*. New York: Pyramid Books, 1950.

Manniche, Lise. *An Ancient Egyptian Herbal*. Austin: University of Texas Press, 1989.

Martin, Laura C. *Garden Flower Folklore*. Old Saybrook, Conn.: Globe Pequot Press, 1987.

Masterson, Ernest W. G. *Hygiene and Disease in Palestine in Modern and in Biblical Times*. London: Palestine Exploration Fund, n.d.

McIntyre, Anne. *Flower Power*. New York: Henry Holt and Co., 1996.

McNutt, Lynn. *Plants of the Holy Lands*. Tucson, Ariz.: Tucson Botanical Gardens, 1998.

Mercatante, Anthony S. *The Magic Garden: The Myth and Folklore of Flowers, Plants, Trees, and Herbs*. New York: Harper and Row, 1976.

Mindell, Earl. *New Herb Bible*. New York: Simon and Schuster, 2000.

Minter, Sue. *The Healing Garden*. Boston: C. E. Tuttle, 1993.

Moldenke, Harold and Alma Moldenke. *Plants of the Bible*. New York: Dover Publications, 1986.

Mullins, Ruth. *Flowers and Symbols for the Christian Year*. New York: Hearthside Press, 1967.

Musselman, Lytton John. *Holy Pharmacy: Modern Medical Uses of Some Plants of the Qu'ran and the Bible: Its Relation to Biodiversity*. Damascus, Syria: American Center, 2000.

Nunn, John F. *Ancient Egyptian Medicine*. Norman, Okla.: University of Oklahoma Press, 1996.

Odijk, Pamela. *The Israelites*. Englewood Cliffs, N.J.: Silver Burdett Press, 1990.

Osborn, Rev. Henry S. *Plants of the Holy Land with Their Fruits and Flowers*. Philadelphia: J. P. Lippincott and Co., 1861.

Packer, James, Merrill Tenney, and William White, eds. *Bible Almanac*. Nashville: Thomas Nelson Publishers, 1980.

_____. *The Land of the Bible*. Nashville: Thomas Nelson Publishers, 1985.

Paterson, John and Katherine Paterson. *Consider the Lilies*. New York: Thomas Y. Crowell, 1986.

Paterson, Wilma. *A Fountain of Gardens, Plants and Herbs of the Bible*. Edinburgh: Mainstream Publishing, 1990.

People's Desk Reference for Essential Oils. Salem, Utah: Essential Science Publishing, 1999.

Powell, Claire. *The Meaning of Flowers*. London: Jupiter Books, 1977.

Reader's Digest. *Magic and Medicine of Plants*. Pleasantville, N.Y.: Reader's Digest Association, Inc., 1986.

Reeves, Carole. *Egyptian Medicine*. Buckinghamshire: Shire Publications, 1992.

Rohde, Eleanour Sinclair. *Garden-craft in the Bible and Other Essays*. Freeport, N.Y.: Books for Libraries Press, 1967.

Roth, Cecil, ed. *Encyclopaedia Judaica*. Jerusalem, Israel: Keter Publishing House Jerusalem, 1972.

Schauss, Hayyim. *The Jewish Festivals*. New York: Schocken Books, 1938.

Shewell-Cooper, W. E. *Plants, Flowers and Herbs of the Bible*. New Canaan, Conn.: Keats Publishing, 1988.

Shuel, Brian. *Guide to Traditional Customs of Britain*. Exeter: Webb and Bower, 1985.

Simmons, Adelma G. *Herb Gardens of Delight*. New York: Hawthorn Books, 1974.

Smith, Debbie. *Israel, the Land*. New York: Crabtree Publishing, 1999.

Squire, David. *The Healing Garden: Natural Healing for Mind, Body, and Soul*. Surrey, U.K.: Contemporary Books, CLB International, 1998.

Steele, Joelle. "And on the Third Day...God Created Herbs," in Faith M. Balsama, *Body and Soul Food from Medjugorje*. Milford, Ohio: Faith Publishing Co., 1996.

Stetter, Cornelius. *The Secret Medicine of the Pharaohs*. Chicago: Edition Q, 1993.

Streep, Peg. *Spiritual Gardening: Creating Sacred Space Outdoors*. Alexandria, Va.: Time-Life Books, 1999.

Swenson, Allan A. *Plants of the Bible and How to Grow Them*. New York: Carol Publishing Group, 1995.

Swerdlow, Joel L. *Nature's Medicine*. Washington, D.C.: National Geographic, 2000.

Thoennes, Kristin. *Israel*. Mankato, Minn.: Bridgestone Books, 1999.

Thomson, William A. R., ed. *Medicines from the Earth: A Guide to Healing Plants*. New York: McGraw-Hill Book Co., 1978.

Thorwald, Jurgen. *Science and Secrets of Early Medicine*. Translated by Richard Winston and Clara Winston. New York: Harcourt Brace and World, 1962.

Tierra, Michael and Candis Cantin. *The Spirit of Herbs*. Stamford, Conn.: U.S. Games Systems, 1993.

Tolhurst, Marilyn. *Israel*. Englewood Cliffs, N.J.: Silver Burdett Press, 1989.

Untermeyer, Louis. *Plants of the Bible*. New York: Golden Press, 1970.

Uval, Beth. *Seder Tu B'Shvat*. Kiryat Ono, Israel: Neot Kedumim, 1998.

Vickery, Roy. *A Dictionary of Plant Lore*. Oxford: Oxford University Press, 1995.

Walker, Winifred. *All the Plants of the Bible*. New York: Harper and Brothers, 1957.

Ward, Kaari, ed. *ABC's of the Bible*. Pleasantville, N.Y.: Reader's Digest Association, Inc., 1991.

Weiss, Gaea and Shandor Weiss. *Growing and Using Healing Herbs*. Emmaus, Penn.: Rodale Press, 1985.

Wigoder, Devorah Emmet. *The Garden of Eden Cookbook*. San Francisco: Harper and Row, 1988.

Wilkinson, John. *The Bible and Healing: A Medical and Theological Commentary*. Grand Rapids, Mich.: Wm. B. Eerdmans, 1998.

Worwood, Valerie Ann. *The Complete Book of Essential Oils and Aromatherapy*. San Rafael, Calif.: New World Library, 1991.

Zohany, Michael. *Plant Life of Palestine: Israel and Jordan*. New York: Ronald Press Co., 1962.

_____. *Plants of the Bible*. Cambridge: Cambridge University Press, 1982.

Index